W9-CBL-030

FIFTY DAYS
PLUS FOREVER

John J. McIlhon

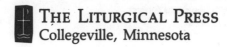
THE LITURGICAL PRESS
Collegeville, Minnesota

Cover by Joshua Jeide, O.S.B.

Nihil obstat: Frank E. Bognanno, *Censor deputatus.*
Imprimatur: ✛ William H. Bullock, D.D., Bishop of Des Moines, January 10, 1990.

1	2	3	4	5	6	7	8	9	10

Library of Congress Cataloging-in-Publication Data

McIlhon, John.
 Fifty days plus forever : daily meditations for Easter / John J.
McIlhon.
  p. cm.
 Includes bibliographical references.
 ISBN 0-8146-1958-4
  1. Eastertide—Meditations. 2. Devotional calendars—Catholic
Church. 3. Catholic Church—Prayer-books and devotions—English.
I. Title. II. Title: 50 days plus forever.
BX2170.E25M3 1990   89-77540
242'.36—dc20   CIP

Contents

Preface

Alleluia is not a word. It is a shout of joy which cannot be expressed in its dictionary meaning. Likewise, the joy of Christ's resurrection cannot be expressed in unborn ages of twenty-four-hour days. Easter's "day the LORD has made" (Ps 118:24) is not only the countless lifetimes in which the mystery of Christ's resurrection is yet to unfold. It is also the eternity necessary for all of humanity to resonate fully with the meaning of Easter's Alleluia. The Church's Easter season is fifty days plus forever.

The Church's seven weeks of Easter's reflections bear witness to the futility of fully expressing Easter's joy. The fifty days of the Church's Easter season can only begin to unfold its mystery and meaning, as Easter's seven weeks of reflection calls us to ponder daily—for the rest of our lives—the joy that awaits us when, led by Christ, we begin to share *here on earth* "the day the LORD has made." On the "day" of our lifetime we are travelers whose pilgrimage is the "passover" from the day of this world's perishability to God's day of imperishability. "This is the day the LORD has made."

This book is the third of a series of daily reflections inviting readers to unite with the Church's universal prayer. Joining Lent's *Forty Days Plus Three* and Advent's *The Lord Is with Us,* this book of Easter reflections retains the format of "Word," "Reflection," and "Questions for Your Reflection." The "Word" is a tiny portion of the Office of Readings taken from the Church's *Liturgy of the Hours.* "Reflection" is the fruit of my own prayerful pondering on the "Word." "Questions for Your Reflection" invites readers to join me as we endeavor to "fill up what is lacking" in Christ's resurrection (Col 1:24).

When Christ was raised from the dead, his risen humanity lacked only our reflection on and our sharing in his risen presence. With Christ, we too must pass over from this world's illusion of perfection in the desert of our perishability to the destiny of imperishability which God created us to become. The pains of that passover pale before the brilliance of resurrection's indescribable joy. This book invites the reader to daily reflections on a joy which a trillion days of Alleluias cannot express. Indeed,

> Eye has not seen, ear has not heard,
>   nor has it so much as dawned on man
>   what God has prepared for those who love him (1 Cor 2:9).

John J. McIlhon

Foreword

Easter is the central mystery of our faith. Yet a central mystery of our lives, ironically, is that we celebrate an Easter faith while we still seek it.

At the conclusion of our Lenten preparations, we come to Easter with hearts renewed, ready for the Alleluias that greet the proclamation of the gospel. Yet we also come to the Easter renewal of our baptismal promises with the growing awareness that we must now take our place alongside the apostles. We, like they, must now witness to what we have seen and heard—the power of God acting in our world, the power of God transforming death into life.

This witness relies on memory. Just as remembering and giving thanks are the essence of our Easter Eucharist, so are they the essence of the witness we are called to give. After a season of remembering the passion of Jesus, our memory of God's power made known in the resurrection changes our lives. However, remembering can be dangerous, as theologian Johann Metz so clearly teaches.[1] Our memories make demands on us, confront us with revealing insights. Our memories help us see more clearly the things with which we have yet to come to terms. This is what gives conviction to our Easter witness. This also becomes a source of hope for our world, because our Easter witness is made known in both words and deeds.

Harvard theologian Margaret Miles describes religion as "a way of seeing." In her book *Image as Insight* she suggests that "it is a way of perceiving a quality of the sensible world in which other human beings and the natural world appear in their full beauty, transformed."[2] This, then, is what the Easter mystery is about. In John McIlhon's words, it is a "hiddenness longing to be revealed."

In *Fifty Days Plus Forever* Monsignor McIlhon shares images from his early years as well as moments from his more recent memory to reveal a lifetime of seeing with the eyes of faith. Like another writing pilgrim, Annie Dillard, his reflections demonstrate a lifelong capacity to "still break through the skin of awareness a thousand times a day."[3]

Is this not what we are invited to in these fifty days of Easter? We celebrate our Easter faith and yet we long to see more clearly.

I thank my friend and former colleague for sharing his faith with me, and for continuing to teach me how the good news invites us to "a new way of seeing . . . through the prism of every created reality."

Sr. Ruth Poochigian, O.P.*

* *Sister Ruth is the director of adult and youth ministries at the St. Joseph Educational Center in West Des Moines, Iowa.*

1. Johann Baptist Metz, *Faith in History and Society: Toward a Practical Fundamental Theology* (New York: Seabury Press, 1980) 66.

2. Margaret R. Miles, *Image as Insight: Visual Understanding in Western Christianity and Secular Culture* (Boston: Beacon Press, 1985) 2.

3. Annie Dillard, *An American Childhood* (New York: Harper and Row, 1987) 250.

For Heaven's Sake, Sing in the Same Key

WORD

"Then Moses and the Israelites sang this song to the
Lord:
I will sing to the Lord, for he is gloriously triumphant"
(Exod 15:1).

REFLECTION

A music teacher left me with an indelible mark of his expertise when he enabled me to understand that music's patterns can become patterns for harmonious living. Under his guidance I discovered that music is not simply something you do; it is also something you become.

One afternoon as we were endeavoring to sing an otherwise lovely song, the "Prof" unceremoniously stopped us in midflight. Hands on hips, he shouted, "For heaven's sake, will you all sing in the same key!"

At the unripe age of ten my curiosity moved me to ask, "Prof, what does it mean to sing in the same key?"

He walked over to the piano, played one note and explained, "The note I am playing is the key of G, and all of the notes in the song belong to G. If some of you, however, decide to sing it in the key of C, this is how it sounds."

What followed was amazing. With his right hand he played the song in the key of G and with his left hand accompanied the melody in the key of C. It had a jarring effect on all of us. Some laughed, some put their hands over their ears, and all of us pleaded with him to stop.

The Prof had made his point. Not only was I motivated to sing on key with the other singers, but later in life I began to ask myself, "What is the keynote at the center of my life?" My music teacher's illustration enabled me to move from music to life in search of life's keynote, around which all of life is harmonized. That search has borne fruit in the conviction that our keynote is the paschal mystery. This pattern of Christ's death and resurrection is the note around which all who relive it "sing on key, for heaven's sake!"

Easter Sunday sounds the key around which the new song of human life has been composed. Those who understand that death and resurrection are the keynote of true life can be sure they are singing on key. To the Romans St. Paul writes: "Are you not aware that we who were baptized into Christ Jesus were baptized into his death? . . . Just as Christ was raised from the dead by the glory of the Father, we too might live a new life" (Rom 6:3-4).

The death of Jesus put to death this world's spirit. But while the voice of this spirit has been silenced, the reverberations of its dissonant song continue to lure the world into singing off key. That song is the lie that the temporalities of the world are the source and summit of humankind's harmony and happiness. Jesus revealed that the basis of all untruthfulness is the world's claim that its perishability is our salvation and glory.

The resurrection of Jesus left no doubt that God's imperishable lordship is the salvation of those destined for eternity. Jesus was sent to establish a new pattern of living whereby we die to a life completely off key to God's purpose for human life. This pattern of life calls for conversion. We are challenged to change from "doing our own thing" to a life of singing, in unison and on key, the new song of the risen Christ's passover pattern for human life.

The psalmist calls us to "sing to the LORD a new song of praise in the assembly of the faithful" (Ps 149:1). This song is a new way of living which arises out of the ashes of this world's cacaphony of off-key notes. Easter is the "day" we are invited to sing this song. It is not a day of twenty-four hours. Easter's day is a competely new way of living whose joyful experience explodes within us in a symphony of songful praise. Easter's day is every day, a reality no longer reckoned by time but reckoned by the peace Christ breathed upon his disciples—the first fruit of his resurrection.

The Easter season challenges us to discernment. If we have died with Christ, do we believe that we are also to live with him (see Rom 6:8)? Do we believe that our lives give evidence that we Christians are singing on key? Is the harmony of our lives, risen with Christ, the judgment against the dissonance of this world's futile, noisy, and empty meanings?

QUESTIONS FOR YOUR REFLECTION

1. The paschal mystery calls us to pass over from the death of one way of living to the resurrection of a new way of living (conversion). How does the kind of Christianity that lives life both ways resemble Prof's playing one song in two different keys? Is that the reason for the "noise" in some people's lives?

2. The spirit of the world embodies the lie that this world can make us happy forever. Why is this lie dangerous to human purpose? In what way does the truth of Christ's paschal mystery restore the life of human purpose?

3. Read Rom 6:3-11. Can you explain how the sacrament of baptism celebrates the paschal mystery? Who is the "old self"? Who is the "new self"? Is it possible for these two selves to sing on key? Explain.

4. It has been said that every Sunday is a "little Easter." How does every "little Easter" necessitate the weekly obligation of singing the "new song" of our faith?

5. The psalmist's assertion that "This is the day the Lord has made" (Ps 118:24) is not about a day of twenty-four hours. What is the Easter meaning of "day"?

Christ's Resurrection: God's Word Kept

WORD

"Praised be the God and Father
of our Lord Jesus Christ,
he who in his great mercy
gave us new birth;
a birth unto hope which draws its life
from the resurrection of Jesus Christ from the dead;
a birth to an imperishable inheritance" (1 Pet 1:3-4).

REFLECTION

The paschal mystery never lets us forget that all of us find ourselves in the midst of a powerful conflict. Because we bear the characteristics of this world, we feel the world's attraction to that which is perishable; because we have been created in the image and likeness of God, we experience our own attraction to that which is imperishable. This unceasing tension can bear the fruits of our dying to the world's attractions and the ecstasy of hope's promise of risen life.

Jesus came to be the sacrament of the paschal mystery. Not for one moment was he free of its tension. His humanity was never spared this world's unceasing assertions of ultimate glory for its display of perishable goods. But neither was he spared the inward groanings of heaven's kingdom calling him to the destiny God created all of humanity to share. From the moment of his conception until his last breath, Jesus lived as humanity's judgment, both of this world's claims of glory and of the truthfulness of God's claims of imperishability.

Jesus' death was neither the failure of God's truthfulness nor of humanity's graced capacity to be faithful to God. The death of Jesus was humanity's greatest moment of glory because, in Christ, the lie that this world's goodness equals God's goodness was put to death. In Christ, humanity put the full weight of its trust in God's claim that its nature had been created for a destiny beyond the world's claims of ultimate goodness.

The death of Jesus was truly "a birth unto hope," dwelling within all who trust it to be the certainty of eternal resurrection. God the Father raised Jesus from death and in that resurrection gave humankind the certainty of imperishability. How joyfully St. Peter cries out:

> From the resurrection of Jesus Christ from the dead;
> [we have] a birth to an imperishable inheritance,
> incapable of fading or defilement" (1 Pet 1: 3-4).

This hope is God's gift to humanity, empowering us with the certainty of our own resurrection. God's gift of hope takes us to the moment of our own death, when birth to the eternal moment of our glory will be the fruit of our trust in God.

Drawing the last breath is not one's only death. Life on earth is a moment-by-moment dying. It is also a moment-by-moment resurrection to the eternity of imperishability. In the midst of this world's perishability, God calls us to experience the beginnings of imperishability. St. Luke writes that Jesus "showed them in many convincing ways that he was alive, appearing to them over the course of forty days and speaking to them about the reign of God" (Acts 1:3). For us, too, it is God's will that evidences of Christ's resurrection be seen in us before we enter the fullness of eternal life.

God's gift of hope is the certainty of resurrection already ours in Christ. St. Peter writes:

> Live soberly; set all your hope on the gift to be conferred on you when Jesus Christ appears. As obedient sons [and daughters], do not yield to the desires that once shaped you in your ignorance. Rather, become holy yourselves in every aspect of your conduct, after the likeness of the holy One who called you; remember, Scripture says, "Be holy, for I am holy" (1 Pet 1:13-16).

Hope, then, guides us with certainty as we make our way on the tension-filled pilgrimage of Christ's paschal mystery. It does not spare us the agony of tension, nor does it cease to promise us the joy of being raised up to an undying destiny. Through Easter's season of joy we have the daily good news of Christ's death and resurrection. Christ's death is humanity's moment of glory; his resurrection is God's Word truly kept in Christ.

QUESTIONS FOR YOUR REFLECTION

1. A memorial acclamation of the Eucharist invites us to pray: "When we eat this bread and drink this cup, we proclaim your death, Lord Jesus, until you come in glory." What commitment does this acclamation summon us to make in our daily lives?

2. The paschal mystery involves the duality of death and resurrection. Why must this be a necessity of human existence?

3. Why is God's gift of hope the certainty of a "happy death"?

4. Saints, like Jesus, live as sacraments of Christ's paschal mystery. In the life of your favorite saint, what are some evidences of his or her commitment to Christ's paschal mystery?

TUESDAY WITHIN THE OCTAVE OF EASTER

Mangled Hands! for Me Too?

WORD

"Only by reflecting upon the meaning of the incarnation can we see how it is possible to say with perfect truth both that Christ suffered and that he was incapable of suffering, and why the Word of God, in himself incapable of suffering, came to suffer" (St. Anastasius of Antioch).[1]

REFLECTION

At age twelve, I found the book *Mangled Hands* deeply moving. Curiously, its story of the North American martyrs both repelled and attracted me. The vicious and violent tortures inflicted by the Iroquois Indians on Sts. Isaac Jogues, John de Brébeuf, and their companions repelled me. Yet, the rocklike certainty which these missionaries resolutely displayed attracted me. *Mangled Hands* opened the door to a meaning of Christ's incarnation well beyond the doctrinal formulation I had so assiduously memorized.

The North American martyrs lived a cruel captivity that to all appearances offered only perishability. Yet they lived in a manner that gave unmistakable evidence of their certainty of life's imperishability. Their witness of this twofold existence quietly and subtly drew me into deeper realms of faith's mystery groaning to be discovered. I little surmised that at age twelve the story of *Mangled Hands* was to lead me to embrace Christ's incarnation and the impact it would have on my life.

Long after reading *Mangled Hands* I asked myself, "Do the North American martyrs represent a curious contradiction between God's incapability of suffering and humanity's capability of suffering?" It struck me that this is really a question about the mystery of Christ's incarnation. It is to this seeming contradiction that St. Anastasius addresses himself: "Only by reflecting upon the meaning of the incarnation can we see how it is possible to say with perfect truth both that Christ suffered and that he was incapable of suffering, and why the Word of God, in himself incapable of suffering, came to suffer."

This seeming contradiction dissolves when faith enables us to see that the incarnation is not contradictory. God created humanity to be the image and likeness of God. But, contrary to the imperishability of humanity's divine purpose, Adam and Eve chose the fruit of perishability as their image and likeness. This choice was at the root of their sinfulness. The only remnant of hope that remained in the depths of humanity's kinship with God was its capability of crying out for salvation. Jesus echoed this longing when he cried out on the cross, "My God, my God, why have you forsaken me?" (Mark 15:34).

The North American martyrs lived Christ's experience of abandonment at the hands of savagery. They also shared Christ's longing for humanity's rightful place in the bosom of God's imperishability. Their longing radiated evidences of faith, hope, and love. America's first martyrs revealed the conviction that these imperishables are incapable of suffering because they empower us to be witnesses of Christ's resurrection.

The Word of God calls us to be martyrs—witnesses—of the imperishability of God's Word, whose seeds promise us indestructibility. These seeds, clothed in the human garments of perishability, must die in the soil of human suffering. Christ witnessed the evidence of humanity's susceptibility to suffering and death, but in so doing he gave witness to humanity's destiny of resurrection. The North American martyrs followed in Christ's footsteps because they believed, trusted, and lovingly

15

embraced Christ's paschal mystery of suffering and dying. By suffering, they gave witness to humanity's capability of suffering, but with their God-given gifts of faith, hope, and love they gave witness to humanity's destiny of sharing eternal life's incapability of suffering.

We too are challenged to believe, trust, and love the truthfulness of the paschal mystery and thereby to accept its invitation to be imperishable. We are called to live Christ's witness of the incarnation, whose capability of suffering we cannot escape but whose promise of an eternity of peace and joy we cannot ignore.

All are not called to the martyrdom of spilling their blood. But all are called to the witness of purging themselves of "everything vicious, everything deceitful; pretenses, jealousies, and disparging remarks of any kind" (1 Pet 2:1). To be purged of these urges is to suffer martyrdom at the hands of a savagery that knows only perishability. But to lay siege with the gifts of faith, hope, and love is to suffer the death of perishability with the peace, joy, and serenity of resurrection's imperishability.

QUESTIONS FOR YOUR REFLECTION

1. In the light of divinity's incapability of suffering, why is Christ's suffering and death not contradictory?

2. How does God's purpose for humanity enable you to understand the seemingly strange alliance of paschal mystery's death and resurrection?

3. How does a reflection on the meaning of the incarnation enable you to "see how it is possible to say with perfect truth both that Christ suffered and that he was incapable of suffering"?

4. The North American martyrs suffered the mangling of their hands. We are challenged to enter deep into the hidden recesses of our hearts. What are we called to "mangle" there (see 1 Pet 2:1)?

Who Is Supposed to Carry out the Garbage?

WORD

> *"Because of the Lord, be obedient to every human institution, whether to the emperor as sovereign or to the governors he commissions for the punishment of criminals and the recognition of the upright. Such obedience is the will of God. You must silence the ignorant talk of foolish men by your good behavior. Live as free men, but do not use your freedom as a cloak for vice. In a word, live as servants of God"* (1 Pet 2:13-16).

REFLECTION

Beginning in the 1960's, the so-called hippy movement began as a model of disestablishment. Young people lived what they perceived to be a communal way of life without the responsibilities of institution's constraints on freedom. The hippy movement failed, it was alleged, when someone asked, "Who is supposed to carry out the garbage?"

Institution is a fact of life. We can no more discard it than we can discard the human body. Human existence is not free when its institutional framework has been disestablished. We are not free outside the boundaries of institution because God has defined us as creatures whose freedom is attained by way of sense experience. Our way to freedom is not the angels' way.

Institution is not the only model of human existence. Its tasks (who is supposed to carry out the garbage?) free us to live with civility and dignity, but these tasks are not the ultimate aims of human existence. When the focus on institutional tasks becomes the only aim of human pursuit we are in danger of becoming enslaved, addicted to a narrow view of freedom.

The Church is defined by way of several models. Institution, however, remains as one important model of her constitution. That's because the Church is human. Her mission to proclaim the good news must be embodied within a framework that enables the Church's membership to receive it, believe it, and live it. Jesus himself, the Son of God, was not dispensed from institution. His embodiment of divinity within human nature committed him to the human manner of accepting God's good news of freedom, believing it, and living it.

Our celebration of Christ's resurrection from the dead is not a celebration of the death of institution. Jesus died at the hands of those who held the institution of *their* time to be the institution for *all* time. The death and resurrection of Jesus celebrated movement, passover, and change. Its mystery continues to call us to the recognition that our relationship with God is not primarily by way of human institution but by way of the person of Jesus. Our vocation is to grow as the human embodiment of Christ *within* the ever-changing features of its ecclesial institution.

When Jesus was raised from the dead, he did not reappear disembodied or disestablished from his humanity. "Why are you disturbed?" Jesus asked the disciples after his resurrection. "Look at my hands and my feet; it is really I. Touch me, and see that a ghost does not have flesh and bones as I do" (Luke 24:38-39). The apostles rejoiced because they saw in Jesus' risen embodiment the beginnings of their own transformed relationship with him and with one another.

The implications of Christ's resurrection in the lives of the apostles ought to be the source of our Easter joy today. We rejoice not because the presence of the risen Christ among us gives us license to deinstitutionalize our ecclesial relationship with Christ but because his risen presence promises a transformation in our ever-changing relatedness to God's image and likeness. This unceasing renewal does not remove the need for institution. Rather, it calls for the renewal of ecclesial institution, whose change enables deeper common understandings of our relationship with God and provides the freedom to journey with one another toward the oneness it envisions.

In every age the Church's pilgrimage is beset by extremists. To her right are those who seek to halt her passover pilgrimage by enthroning her in the chair of institution's immutable triumphalism. To her left are those who seek to enthrone her in the chair of freedom's triumphant disengagement from institution. When the Church rejects the claims of both extremes she receives their denunciations, which enables her to carry the cross of Christ's pilgrimage. This painful experience is embraced in the joy of the resurrection, the source of the Church's pilgrimage.

Those who journey the passover of salvation with Christ follow Peter, whom he instituted to be his first vicar-shepherd. It is Peter who writes, "I urge you not to indulge your carnal desires. By their nature they wage war on the soul. . . . Because of the Lord, be obedient to every human institution, . . . Such obedience is the will of God" (1 Pet 2:11, 13, 15).

QUESTIONS FOR YOUR REFLECTION

1. What are some of the institutions within family life that provide family members with common understandings for peaceful living?

2. For over two thousand years the Church has displayed the flexibility of existing in a variety of social, political, economic, and cultural forms. In what way would a refusal to be flexible with her own institutional model prevent the Church from being truly catholic?

3. Suppose a hypothetical Vatican Council III would turn the Church back to her pre-Vatican II institutional form. In such a reversal, who would be the new progressives and the new traditionalists?

4. The risen Christ continues to be present among us by way of an institutional Church. Why didn't Jesus choose to be among us universally by way of apparitions rather than institutions?

Why Do You Hope in Your Baptism?

WORD

"Who indeed can harm you if you are committed deeply to doing what is right? Even if you should have to suffer for justice' sake, happy will you be. 'Fear not and do not stand in awe of what this people fears.' Venerate the Lord, that is, Christ, in your hearts. Should anyone ask you the reason for this hope of yours, be ever ready to reply, but speak gently and respectfully" (1 Pet 3:13-16).

REFLECTION

The weekly visits of three young brothers made one of my summers in a small rural parish memorable. Instruction in the Catholic faith was the purpose of their visits, for which we gathered beneath a huge elm tree. Unwittingly, those visits also became the source of *my* instruction in the Catholic faith.

My enlightenment began one afternoon with a lad's utterly simple question about the sacrament of baptism. "Father," he asked, "Why do you hope in your baptism?" His question somewhat chastised me for not heeding St. Peter's exhortation: "Should anyone ask you the reason for this hope of yours, be ever ready to reply." I cannot remember one word of my answer to that little boy, but I have never forgotten his question.

It is not by accident that the Church designates the First Epistle of Peter as nourishment for those who pray the daily Liturgy of the Hours for the octave of Easter. Easter's prayer and reflection invites us to join many newly baptized catechumens who are exhorted by the Church to have their answer ready for people who "ask . . . the reason [of their] hope." It is likewise not by accident that I invite you to join me as I continue to answer the small boy's question: "Why do you hope in your baptism?"

After their baptism first-century catechumens spent a long period of time reflecting on baptism's meaning in their lives. They too were led to ask themselves for the reason of their hope. Their postbaptismal catechesis began:

> You were led down to the font of holy baptism just as Christ was taken down from the cross and placed in the tomb which is before your eyes. Each of you was asked, "Do you believe in the name of the Father, and of the Son, and of the Holy Spirit?" You made the profession of faith that brings salvation, you were plunged into the water, and three times you rose again. This symbolized the three days Christ spent in the tomb.[2]

In what way did these words offer the newly baptized a reason for baptism's hope? The answer lies in their threefold profession of faith "in the name of the Father, and of the Son, and of the Holy Spirit." By this profession of faith in God's trinitarian personhood, they embraced faith's certainty that humanity's purpose of existence flows from God's identity. To believe in the name of God's triune personhood meant a total commitment to a way of life commensurate with the God-likeness humanity was created to become.

It is the same with us. Baptism challenges all of us to measure our lives by the God-like reality that cannot perish. The death we are asked to embrace at baptism is our renunciation of a way of life measured by the perishable criteria of this world. The things of this world, necessary as they are *for this life,* are not the hope of baptism. To be baptized in the hope that God will bless us with an abundance of what this world offers is to seek futility. To embrace baptism with the hope of fulfilling our creaturehood's likeness to God's triune image is to seek a transformation into the likeness of Christ's resurrection.

Baptism challenges us to die to the futility of the world's promises. It also calls us to expect the resurrection of the imperishable destiny that cannot be fully experienced or described here on earth. Baptism is our passover experience from death to resurrection, by which we "fill up what is lacking in the sufferings of Christ" (Col 1:24) in our daily lives.

Easter's message of hope is not pretty words for pious ears. It is a message calling us to renew our paschal pilgrimage from sensuality's life of futility to sacramentality's life of companionship with God the Father, God the Son, and God the Holy Spirit. This is the hope—the certainty—of the companionship that baptism invites us to profess, count on, and love. This is the life to which God the Father commissioned Jesus as Savior for humankind. This is the life Jesus, after his ascension, "poured out in our hearts by the Holy Spirit" (Rom 5:5), calling us to be wholly one with God. To be wholly one with God's trinitarian personhood is to be holy. That's the hope baptism holds for me!

QUESTIONS FOR YOUR REFLECTION

1. What is the reason for your hope in the sacrament of baptism?

2. When "symbol" becomes synonomous with "token," what damage does this erosion of meaning inflict on the reality that symbols celebrate? What is the daily lived reality of baptism? For example, what responsibility does the baptism of infants make imperative for parents?

3. Recall a person whose life has demonstrated for you a consistency between baptism's symbol and its lived reality. How would you tell that person's story at a parish catechumenate gathering?

4. How would you compare the meaning of "passover" with the meaning of "conversion"? Why do we associate pilgrimage with both words?

FRIDAY WITHIN THE OCTAVE OF EASTER

"You still do not know me"

WORD

"As generous distributors of God's manifold grace, put your gifts at the service of one another" (1 Pet 4:10).

REFLECTION

Until I visited the monastery of Monte Cassino in southern Italy I did not know that its founder, St. Benedict, and his sister, St. Scholastica, were buried there. This belated discovery became a moment of grace as I knelt before their resting place. The magnitude of their influence over fifteen centuries astonished me. I knelt in wonder at the power that extended their felt presence to attract thousands of men and women to the discipleship of their rule of life, even to this day.

That moment of wonder in the crypt beneath the monastery led me to wonder about the source of these saints' continuing influence. I was graced to understand that the source of their continuing attraction is the power of Christ's death and resurrection. The good news of the paschal mystery is its availability to all of us who trust its capacity to transform and make us "distributors of God's manifold grace." This is the power that is timeless.

My visit to Monte Cassino many years ago continues to be a source of reflection each season of Easter. This holy season makes available to us the transforming power of Christ's risen presence in our midst. His redemptive power does not require the historical repitition of his death and resurrection. "The reason why Christ died for sins once for all," St. Peter writes, was because he "was given life in the realm of the spirit" (1 Pet 3:18). The saving act of Christ's "once for all" death and resurrection brought the Holy Spirit into the world to become the active and effective power of Christ's paschal mystery.

Christians are called to be a surprising people not only because they have renounced "lives of debauchery, evil desires, drunkenness, orgies, carousing, and wanton idolatry" (1 Pet 4:3) but also because their lives give witness to the marvels that create surprise among those who see no other meaning of human existence. First-century catechumens were reminded of this:

> When we were baptized into Christ, and clothed ourselves in him, we were transformed into the image and likeness of God. . . . God gave us a likeness in his glory, and living as we do in communion with Christ, God's anointed, we ourselves are rightly called "the anointed ones." When he said, "Do not touch my anointed ones," he was speaking to us.[3]

As Christ's glory transforms us, we are anointed to be witnesses to God's surprising marvels: healing, reconciliation, peace, mercy, and forgiveness. We are anointed by Christ's glory to "put [our] gifts at the service of one another." The power of Christ's paschal mystery engages us *now*. Its story cannot remain only in the pages of history and the manuals of theology if its power is to be effective in our lives. We too are history; we too are theology's faith seekers, searching the mysteries of faith for understanding. The power of Christ's redemption is available first and foremost through the Holy Spirit's transforming action in our lives. Nothing needs to stand between God's Spirit and "ourselves [who] are rightly called 'the anointed ones.'"

Time's offering of communion with Sts. Benedict and Scholastica has remained untouched for over fifteen hundred years because they let the spirit of God anoint their lives as they lived the paschal mystery. That anointing has reached out beyond their consecrated lives to touch thousands of men and women who have been attracted to their rule of life. Indeed, the communion of saints is not a figure of speech!

God is not surprised at who we can be and what we can do in Christ. God is surprised only that *we* are surprised by the effects of the Spirit's transforming power in our lives. Jesus reflected God's surprise when he said to Philip, "after I have been with you all this time, you still do not know me?" (John 14:9). Jesus did not come to tell us *about* God. He came to offer us God's intimacy: to anoint us, transform us, and make us witnesses of God's marvels in our time. The presence of saints remains not in monuments of stone and marble but in the wonders of compassion, healing, mercy, and peace, which no crypt can hide from God's transforming Spirit.

QUESTIONS FOR YOUR REFLECTION

1. Who is your favorite saint? What is his or her "monument" of holiness that motivates you to reflect Christ's paschal mystery in your own life?

2. When we make a break with "lives of debauchery, evil desires, drunkenness, orgies, carousing, and wanton idolatry," what surprising way of living might we expect from our new identity (see Gal 5:22-23)?

3. What is the difference between the memory of saints in the pages of history and the communion of saints in one's daily life?

4. In what way are sacraments the effective instruments of keeping alive the memory, communion, and power of Christ's paschal mystery in every age? What demand does every sacrament make of us?

The Kingdom of Heaven Is Like Soil, Seeds, and Sowing

WORD

"You have been taught and you are firmly convinced that what looks and tastes like bread and wine is not bread and wine but the body and blood of Christ" (Jerusalem Catechesis).[4]

REFLECTION

I do not doubt that apparitions happen. I do doubt them to be foundational for one's spirituality. This doubt arises from my belief that the ordinariness of creation serves as a sacrament of Christ's presence. A world that "is charged with the grandeur of God"[5] hardly needs apparitions as the cornerstone of spirituality.

One balmy spring evening I knelt beside my father as he planted a row of radish seeds. "Is that where radishes come from?" my six-year-old mind wanted to know. "Well," he laughed, "radishes come from God but we have to plant the seeds." Handing them to me, and under his watchful eye, I finished planting what would later come from God.

My first garden experience left me astonished that ordinary seeds, soil, and sowing could be instruments of God's power and presence. I remember no better lesson about the presence of God in my life than that first garden experience. My father's catechesis with his "textbook" of seeds, soil, and sowing became the foundation of a spirituality that invited me to look with the eyes of faith for the hidden grandeur of God that charges all of creation. I fell in love with gardening not only because it gave promise of food but also because it awakened my faith to see creation as a sacrament of God's presence in the world.

All creation groans to reveal God's identity. St. Paul puts it this way: "I consider the sufferings of the present to be as nothing compared with the glory to be revealed in us. Indeed, the whole created world eagerly awaits the revelation of the [children] of God" (Rom 8:18-19).

The seven sacraments herald God's creation as the medium through which God's presence is revealed to the world. My garden experience with ordinary things as instruments of God's presence enabled me to grasp the sacramental simplicity of bread, wine, water, and oil as signs of both divine presence and creation's significance. The sacraments' use of creation's simplicity enabled me to have a deep respect and reverence for the significance of creation as sacrament of God's appearance to the eyes of faith.

Dubious, however, is the spirituality that assigns sacredness *only* to those created goods blessed for sacred use. This separation of "blessed" and "not blessed" creates an artificial frame of reference that holds only the blessed as good—and the secular as bad. As long as this schizophrenic approach to creation prevails, the seven sacraments will hardly achieve passover's conversion of head and heart. Intellectual assent to Christ's healing presence only in sacred symbols will encourage hungry hearts to seek apparitions outside his presence.

Faith calls obedient minds and hearts to bless all of creation with the recognition that everything is sacred. When God spoke to Moses from the burning bush, God exclaimed, "the place where you stand is holy ground" (Exod 3:5). If faith is truly alive, spirituality doesn't need to rest on a foundation of apparitions somewhere "up in the sky" or "across the sea" (Deut 30:11-14). Faith that accepts with both heart and head the orthodoxy of Christ's sacramental presence in the created elements of bread and wine will never be comfortable with the belief that creation is separated into the sacred and the secular. Faith becomes inconsistent when one believes that while Christ is present in a church, one needs to travel "across the sea" to see an apparition on "holy ground" away from home.

To see the presence of Christ on the "holy ground" of creation is to raise creation from the ordinariness of its subservience of supplying humanity's earthly needs to its obedience of revealing to the eyes of faith God's truth, goodness, and beauty. My father's garden catechized me to go beyond my body's relish for radishes to the presence of God, with God's call to relish creation's companionship.

In the first century catechumens were asked "not [to] regard the eucharistic elements as ordinary bread and wine [but as] the body and blood of the Lord."[6] Today the resurrection of Christ continues to take place within a Eucharistic frame of reference. The Eucharist's sacramentality never ceases to send us to "the whole created world [as it] eagerly awaits the revelation of the [children] of God" (Rom 8:19). It is our search for the presence of God in creation's ordinariness that calls forth the risen presence of Christ from both creation's ordinariness and ours.

QUESTIONS FOR YOUR REFLECTION

1. Reflecting on your past life, what are some ordinary experiences that revealed to you the presence of God?

2. Respect for life requires that we be consistent. What is to be said about the inconsistency of being anti-abortion and pro–capital punishment? Who is supposed to separate the good and the bad (see Matt 25:31-46)?

3. The seven sacraments make effective what they signify. What does this promise hold for those who have a deep respect and reverence for creation?

4. In the light of the sacraments' significance, why is consumerism a deformity of human dignity? Why is consumerism the enemy of Christ's paschal mystery?

SUNDAY WITHIN THE OCTAVE OF EASTER

Our Sacrament of Solidarity

WORD

"Since you have been raised up in company with Christ, set your heart on what pertains to higher realms where Christ is seated at God's right hand. Be intent on things above rather than on things of earth" (Col 3:1-2).

REFLECTION

My father lost his job during the Great Depression. For two years our family experienced poverty. But those years also deepened our family's experience of solidarity.

Among my possessions there is one which I call the "sacrament of our family solidarity." It is a cereal bowl in which we children placed all of our meager earnings needed for groceries. This very ordinary dish gradually became a sign of sharing, whose bonds of love and compassion enabled the strength of our family solidarity to be revealed.

Now in its sixtieth year, the bowl is sacred because its presence puts me in touch again and again with the sacredness that it signifies. For over sixty years, this very ordinary dish has enabled me to keep the eyes of faith fixed on the role of this world's possessions as mediators of God's love and generosity. I am reminded that the sacredness of possessions is not their materiality but their capacity to be sacraments of values that transcend their material substance. To set our hearts only on the possession of material things with the illusion that they provide us with a transcendent worth is a worth control that severs us from God.

"Be intent on things above rather than on things of earth." St. Paul does not repudiate the goodness of material things. Rather, he calls us to raise our hearts and minds to the "higher realms" of their significance. The glory of this world's creaturehood does not reside exclusively in the value of its substance. Its glory unfolds when our capacity to see the sacred reality of "higher realms" calls it forth.

The glory of bread and wine's Eucharistic creaturehood is the sacramental dignity to which Christ raised it. By changing its material substance into Christ's Body and Blood, Christ raised bread and wine to the "higher realms" of his identity. It was of bread and wine that Jesus said to his disciples, "This is my body, which is for you. . . . This cup is the new covenant in my blood" (1 Cor 11:24-25). By changing bread and wine into his Body and Blood, Christ proclaimed the dignity of all creaturehood in its capacity to be sacramental of God's presence, which faith also calls us to become.

The purpose of the seven sacraments is not to separate the designated sacredness of their material substance from all other materiality. Their sacramental sacredness invites us to see the sacredness of all creation. For example, the sacredness of the Eucharist's food and drink is not only that of their transformed substance but also their capacity to signify creation's role to be Christ's refreshing nourishment for those who hunger and thirst for God's "higher realms."

In his Epistle to the Romans St. Paul writes, "Creation was made subject to futility, not of its own accord but by him who once subjected it" (8:20). The futility of creation lies not in its materiality but in the illusion that it provides us with ultimate worth. Created goods are rendered futile when their blessing is reckoned only by the satisfaction their use provides. When this purpose is perceived to be their sole purpose, "Creation [remains] subject to futility." When materialistic attitudes render creation's sacramentality futile, they blind us to God's longing for our resurrection.

Creation's blessedness invites us to embrace human worth as God sees it. Creation's goodness "groans" for us to look beyond its materiality to the worth God blessed us to become: blessed to be like God, blessed to be children of God, blessed to be seated with Christ at God's right hand for all eternity. No earthly good possesses a worth commensurate with this. But all of this earth's goods possess the worth of beckoning us to embrace their imperishable significance.

QUESTIONS FOR YOUR RELECTION

1. When we seek the significance of anything, aren't we really searching for its "higher realms" of meaning? For example, beyond its chemical composition of hydrogen and oxygen, what higher realms of meaning does water symbolize (see John 4:4-24)?

2. Contemplation is the prayer that graces us to be conscious of our communion with God. How does the sacramentality of ordinary things invite us to higher realms of prayer?

3. What very ordinary possession do you hold sacred? Why do you fear its loss?

4. There are many sins, but one sinfulness. In view of the attitude that regards the role of material things to be no more than pleasurable gratification, what would you say is the sinfulness at the root of all sins?

Alpha and Omega: Humanity's Purpose

WORD

"This is the revelation God gave to Jesus Christ, that he might show his servants what must happen very soon. He made it known by sending his angel to his servant John, who in reporting all he saw bears witness to the word of God and the testimony of Jesus Christ" (Rev 1:1-2).

REFLECTION

At birth, there is available to us a myriad of symbols that point to life's meaning. In the beginning we understand none of them, but their repitition gradually unfolds meanings that awaken human nature's social instincts. At length we come to understand love's role as the center focus and purpose of human life.

There is little disagreement about the difficulty of understanding Sacred Scripture's final book, Revelation. This book, also called the Apocalypse, possesses a symbolism that veils a "coded" message which first-century Christians in danger of martyrdom found familiar. Within the imagery of its symbols lay hidden the good news which Christ's death and resurrection had already revealed—that we are loved by God! We are loved so fully that we were created to live for no other purpose than to become the likeness of that love.

The difficulty of understanding the book's imagery is our preoccupation with its mystery. This preoccupation is not much more than scriptural autism, which displays perfect fidelity to the pieces rather than to their wholeness. John, Revelation's author, sees the wholeness of humanity's purpose and veils it with "coded" imagery. Its message, for those with eyes to see and ears to hear (see Matt 13:15), contains the wholeness of salvation's picture: "I am the Alpha and the Omega, the One who is and who was and who is to come, the Almighty!" (Rev 1:8). By means of these words, the Lord revealed to John humankind's only purpose for existence. Like newborn children, the readers of John's Revelation came to understand, through the apocalyptic imagery of the

Greek alphabet's first and last letters, that God was the beginning and the end of human life's purpose and meaning.

This world cannot offer ultimate meaning for human existence any more than can the unborn's umbilical cord, severed at birth because its wombed purpose has ended. Revelation's message is the joy that *never-ending* salvation is already ours. It is yet to come only to the extent that we remain attached to the umbilical cord of the world's claims to be life's only meaning.

When Christ died on the cross he cut the umbilical cord of the world's false claims. When God raised Jesus' humanity to the newness of his transfiguration, there was made available to us the certainty of our own transfiguration, signified by Christ's death and resurrection. Jesus' paschal mystery reveals to us the passover pilgrimage—the meaning of John's message in Revelation.

An ancient Easter homily attributed to St. John Chrysostom declares:

> Christ . . . puts an end to our former life, and through the regenerating waters of baptism in which we imitate his death and resurrection, he gives us the beginning of a new life. The knowledge that Christ is the Passover lamb who was sacrificed for us should make us regard the moment of his immolation as the beginning of our own lives. . . . Having once understood it, we should enter upon this new life with all eagerness and never return to the old one, which is not at an end."[7]

For four of Easter's seven weeks the Church invites us to reflect on the meaning of Revelation. This book calls us to enter the darkness of its apocalyptic imagery so that faith may lead us to the radiance of Christ's life as the Alpha and the Omega of our existence. Just as we may never gaze directly at the sun without the prism of darkly colored glass, so the Book of Revelation offers us darkly coded prisms of apocalyptic imagery with which to perceive glimpses of heaven's radiance already ours. The joy of these glimpses is the indescribable good news that their radiance can be witnessed by those who see in the followers of Christ conclusive evidence that God is humanity's Alpha and Omega.

QUESTIONS FOR YOUR REFLECTION

1. The final book of the Bible is about a revelation that has already been made but is yet to come. Using the example of the birth of

a baby, how is this "already–not yet" apparent contradiction reconciled?

2. John reveals that God is the Alpha (beginning) and the Omega (end) of human existence. What other "alphas" and "omegas" of human existence does this world's message of "salvation" endeavor to sell us in the media? Give some examples.

3. For those who subscribe to another "ultimate" reason for human existence, why does Christ's Passover experience no longer seem appropriate to their way of living? What about the remark "I no longer get anything out of my religion"?

4. If conversion is the decision to embrace God as the Alpha and the Omega of human purpose, what must be severed if conversion is to have the effect of transforming one's human existence?

TUESDAY OF THE SECOND WEEK

Freedom to Perish?

WORD

"Have no fear of the sufferings to come" (Rev 2:10).

REFLECTION

Freedom is not the license to possess. To spend our lives in the pursuit of having under the illusion that possessions will make us fully free produces only the fruit of possessing perishability.

A sign of our addiction to perishability is the fear that without having we will be without being. This fear is the beginning of fears. Cardinal Joseph Bernardin writes, "In a consumer-oriented society, we need to remind each person that our worth derives from who we are rather than what we own."[8]

God did not create the goodness of this world to be the ultimate form of human identity. God created perishables to serve humankind's temporary tenure in this world. While we live here we have needs that cease when the need to breathe ceases. No worldly goodness is needed when we enter eternal life.

God created human life for the imperishability of eternal life. Although humankind was created kin to earth's perishability, it was also created kin to heaven's imperishability. It is at this juncture that we find imperative the suffering of the passover pilgrimage which takes us from one identity to another.

We fear suffering because we fear losing the identity which this world's perishables can so easily form. The identity which faith offers is difficult to grasp because its imagery is difficult to imagine. This is not to say that one's perishable possessions are the enemies of faith. But they become enemies when their possession creates an illusion of perfect happiness with the identity which that illusion forms.

Writing to the Church at Smyrna, John voices the Lord's exhortation: "Have no fear of the sufferings to come. . . . I will give you the crown of life" (Rev 2:10). This crown, this epitome of human life's existence, is the full sharing of God's life in its alpha and omega meaning. In the Book of Revelation, John invites the Church at Smyrna to make the paschal pilgrimage from this world's perishable identity to God's imperishability. John's deep faith moves him to consider that no anxiety about losing this world's goods outweighs the peace and joy of being God's imperishability.

God longs for humanity to become the likeness of God's imperishability. Nothing is more loathsome to God than the perversion of our settling for this world's perishability as the alpha and omega of human purpose. Our reason for gathering frequently around the altar is to be reminded of human destiny's imperishability. We are invited to discern again and again our relationship with God in a world where perishables vie to be humankind's alpha and omega.

God created us for a freedom that transcends the temporary pleasures of this earth. The freedom to be rather than to have is worth the suffering all of us are called to embrace as we travel the paschal pilgrimage of Christ's death and resurrection. This is the sacrifice we are all called to live, the sacrifice of Christ who daily longs for us to "fill up what is lacking in the sufferings of Christ for the sake of his body, the church" (Col 1:24). We who make up the body of Christ *become* sacraments of Christ's sacrifice. The Eucharist is our celebration of that sacred reality, a reality that must be lived!

St. Fulgentius of Ruspe writes: "God makes the Church itself a sacrifice pleasing in his sight by preserving within it the love which the Holy Spirit has poured out. Thus the grace of that spiritual love is always available to us, enabling us continually to offer ourselves to God as a living sacrifice, holy and pleasing to him forever."[9]

Sacrifice is never easy, nor is it easy to put faith in the choice of imperishability as *the* way of living. Yet faith is freedom's doorway. It calls for the freedom of leaving the identity of our possessions to become the identity of God's image and likeness. This passage is our lifetime pilgrimage of sacrifice. When we experience that passover pilgrimage, we shall understand what St. Paul means when he writes:

> Eye has not seen, ear has not heard
>   nor has it so much as dawned on man
>   what God has prepared for those who love him (1 Cor 2:9).

QUESTIONS FOR YOUR REFLECTION

1. In what way is Christ's death and resurrection his "declaration of independence"? From what dependence are we freed?

2. While we live in this world we are subject to perishable needs: food, clothing, housing. At what point does our freedom to possess these necessities become a threat to God's purpose for human existence?

3. While suffering is never easy, it is imperative that we embrace it. Why? How does God's gift of faith enable us to make that embrace willingly and unconditionally?

4. What is the basic reason we fear suffering? How does our confusion about the meaning of freedom promote fear?

God's Word: The Two-Edged Sword

WORD

"The One with the sharp, two-edged sword has this to say: . . ." (Rev 2:12).

REFLECTION

We expect healing from surgeons. We also expect pain. Surgeons must cut before they can heal.

And so it is with God's Word. Its "two-edged sword" makes an incision where sinfulness has fractured the wholeness of our being. The strength of the Word's healing lies in its power to restore us to our wholeness with God's identity.

The Book of Revelation begins with its author's mission to the seven Churches of Asia Minor. John was commissioned by "the One with the sharp, two-edged sword" to bring them God's healing peace as well as the pain of excising the sinfulness that destroys peace. He showed each of the Churches where their faith was strong and where it was weak so that they might bear witness to Christ's Passover victory.

He wrote not to seven independent Church bodies but to a body of interdependent communions whose head, Jesus Christ, is the head of all ecclesial communion. This is the head who commissioned him to bring the two-edged sword of pain and healing to the one body of Christ. The Church's virtue is Christ's glory, but her sinfulness is Christ's suffering. His intimacy with the members of his body has made imperative the pain of his double-edged Word.

St. Leo the Great writes: "There is no doubt that the Son of God took our human nature into so close a union with himself that one and the same Christ is present, not only in the firstborn of all creation, but in his saints as well. The head cannot be separated from the members, nor the members from the head."[10]

St. Leo adds that Christ's healing is "not for us simply a matter of past history [for] here and now we experience his power at work among us."[11] Yes, after two thousand years, John's deep concern for the ecclesial health of Asia Minor's seven Churches has reached across the centuries to touch the communion of our own ecclesial identity. Today he offers us the Word's "two-edged sword" to exalt virtue and excise sin. God's Word sees evidence of the Church's compassion, mission-mindedness, martyrdom, and prophetic courage throughout the world. These virtues form and shape our unity and its witness to God's triune communion. God's Word also sees evidence of a false unity springing from the observance of externals without the observance of their inner meaning. Religion by externals only opens the way to a loss of the sense of sin and the inconsistency of an ethic that picks and chooses what is right and wrong. Adherence to the uniformity of religion by externals generates the illusion that ecclesial communion is secure.

The two-edged sword of God's Word does not promise adherents of pick-and-choose morality any healing until they let its cutting edge penetrate the depths of their reason for human existence. To the Church of Thyatira the Son of God spoke words of pain before he became the Word of healing: "Thus shall all the churches come to know that I am the searcher of hearts and minds, and that I will give each of you what your conduct deserves" (Rev 2:23).

The loss of the sense of sin is tragic because it empowers its victims to reject God's incision. The "searcher of hearts and minds" seeks not to condemn but to arouse repentance. The tragedy of the loss of a sense of sin is that it becomes the barrier to God's gift of healing.

Cardinal Joseph Bernardin's *Consistent Ethic of Life* exposes the inconsistency of pick-and-choose morality: "A consistent ethic of life is based on the need to ensure that the sacredness of human life, which is the ultimate source of human identity, will be defended and fostered from womb to tomb, from the genetic laboratory to the cancer ward, from the ghetto to the prison."[12]

This "consistent ethic of life" is a seamless garment whose wholeness embraces many areas of ethical concern. To pick and choose one of them as the totality of all morality is unjust and immoral. It goes without saying that before the diseases of any moral issue can be healed, the underlying disease of the loss of a sense of sin, with its tolerance of an inconsistent ethic of picking and choosing, needs attention.

The author of Revelation addresses himself to an ethical inconsistency which he sees in the Church at Thyatira. While he approves of her deeds of love and faith and service (see Rev 2:19), he also warns against her easy tolerance of "a Jezebel" who "refuses to turn from her

36

lewdness" (Rev 2:20-21). This Church of potential greatness gave clear evidence of the inner disease of silence, which indicted her for her responsibility in consenting to evil conduct in her midst.

Our oneness with the first-century's Church is likewise a seamless garment. What the bearer of the Word's two-edged sword did not tolerate cannnot be tolerated at any time. John's plea to Thyatira is a plea to us: "Let him [or her] who has ears heed the Spirit's word to the churches!" (Rev 2:29).

QUESTIONS FOR YOUR REFLECTION

1. What is the danger of tolerating in silence the presence of sin behind the facade of an ethic of picking and choosing what is right and wrong? What is the danger of the attitude that says, "To each his own"?

2. What is your understanding of "the loss of a sense of sin"?

3. How does a pick-and-choose sense of morality bring about today's complaints concerning the practice of double-standard moral behavior?

4. When one converts to the perspective of "a consistent ethic of life," what change of ethical attitude must one make about right and wrong?

THURSDAY OF THE SECOND WEEK

Prayer: The Door That Opens from Within

WORD

"Here I stand, knocking at the door. If anyone hears me calling and opens the door, I will enter his house and have supper with him, and he with me" (Rev 3:20).

REFLECTION

We cannot initiate intimacy with God. Only God begins the friendship and companionship that is our salvation. God's longing for our intimacy is the substance of God's prayer. We pray well when we respond to God's longing to share our companionship. Indeed, prayer is our response to God's longing to be at home in us.

Prayer springs from God's identity. "God is love. . . . Love, then, consists in this: not that we have loved God but that he has loved us" (1 John 4:8, 10). Prayer is God's longing for us to open the wholeness of our personhood for the restoration of the companionship between heaven and earth.

To the Church at Laodicea, God speaks through John: "Here I stand, knocking at the door. If anyone hears me calling and opens the door, I will enter his house and have supper with him, and he with me." This is God's view of prayer. From that perspective, prayer is our openness to the many ways God is knocking on the doors of our lives. Prayer is God's deepest longing, thirst, hunger, and I daresay, agony that we enjoy the presence of heaven's intimacy within us.

Our role in prayer is what God asks of the flock at Laodicea: Hear me calling. To pray well is to listen well. The vocation of prayer—it *is* vocation—is to perceive the diversity of ways God seeks our attention. The essence of prayer is not to get God's attention (we have it) but that God might get our attention (God doesn't have it).

We don't hear God because we are making too much noise praying for God's attention. We storm heaven with prayers while God waits for us to hear his gentle whisperings. It is not true that God keeps us waiting. It *is* true that God waits for the silence that enables us to hear the Word.

God is the God of silence. Elijah discovered this after he received the courage and the strength to walk "forty days and forty nights to the mountain of God, . . ." (1 Kgs 19:8). There he discovered that God's presence is not in wind, earthquake, or fire. God led Elijah to experience heaven's awesome presence in a "tiny whispering sound" (1 Kgs 19:12). He had been raised from the near despair of getting God's attention to the joy of being attentive to God's whispered longings. He found strength in the tiny sound that allowed him to hear God's longing for companionship.

Are there "tiny whispering sounds" in our lives? Yes, all around us! They whisper persistently and imploringly in a diversity of voices, as numerous as the grains and the grapes of Christ's whispering Eucharistic presence. Their presence calls us to the diversity of pleadings from the impoverished voices of those who echo Christ's words: "As often as you did it for one of my least [ones] you did it for me" (Matt 25:40).

In the silence of daily prayer we begin to notice God pleading for us to hear the voices of poverty in our midst. This was the point of Jesus' parable about Lazarus and the rich man. Lazarus begged for a tiny share of food from the rich man's splendid feast, but he received from the floor only scraps that the rich man shared with the dogs. Lazarus begged for the rich man to hear poverty's "whispering sound." The rich man didn't even notice.

We too fail to hear Christ's "tiny whispering sound" not because we are evil but because we are making too much noise pounding on God's door. What foolishness! God's door is already open because Jesus came as heaven's way, truth, and life. That trinity of God's openness will never be closed to us. It is we who are closed to God. Prayer is God's whispering to us: "Here I stand, knocking at the door. If anyone hears me calling and opens the door, I will enter his house and have supper with him, and he with me."

QUESTIONS FOR YOUR REFLECTION

1. All of humanity was created for the intimacy of communion with God and one another. Where does this communion begin? How does it begin?

2. True prayer transforms us. How is God's perspective of prayer a part of that transformation? Describe the change in identity that God's perspective of prayer can bring about.

3. Why does God prefer to speak to us in a "tiny whispering sound"?

4. If the Church were judged by God to have a bias, why would God prefer that it be biased toward the poor?

Christ's Cross Is Heaven's Door

WORD

"Come up here and I will show you what must take place in time to come" (Rev 4:1).

REFLECTION

When we open the doors of our lives to Christ, we enable him to open the door of his life to us. The life of Christ is the fullness of heaven. The reign of Christ is the reign of heaven already in our midst (see Luke 17:21).

Faith is the way we experience the presence of heaven here on earth. That experience is beyond our human capacity to grasp and express. Faith is the prism that enables us to embrace heaven's presence and its gift of transformation.

When we invite Christ to be at home within, we welcome all of heaven. That is the dignity only faith can discern. For that reason the full awareness of why we possess human dignity rests on faith, which fills up what is lacking in our inability to be fully aware of heaven's presence in the mystery of Christ's ongoing incarnation.

There are times, however, when the prism of faith is accompanied by glimpsed experiences of heaven. Occasionally God offers appearances of heaven that allow people to see visual images of the heavenly presence that all of us are called to see with faith. These visions offered to the naked eye cannot be described except by analogies that defy understanding. Yet how can one describe a vision of heaven with earthly analogies that are too shallow for the glory of heaven?

The Book of Revelation is filled with John's earthly imagery, which does fall short of being able to describe his heavenly experience. That is not an indictment against John. It is an indictment against the possibility of describing a visual experience to which only faith can assent. How does one describe the beauty of a sunset for one born blind?

A preoccupation with the imagery of Revelation is futile in the face of our inability to measure heaven's truth with earth's values. The Book of Revelation does not call us to ignore our inabilities. It invites our inabilities to embrace the tree of Christ's cross. "Come up here and I will show you what must take place in time to come." The tree of Christ's cross opens for us faith's way of putting us in touch with the fruits of Christ's resurrection as we journey toward our risen destiny.

Christ's death on the tree of his cross gives evidence that the world's possessions have no power to discern the mystery of life. Christ's cross does not give rebirth to futility. Its poverty gives birth to humanity's fullest sharing in heaven's glory. Three days after he was buried, Christ was raised from the dead. His risen and transformed humanity testifies that God accepts Christ's death not as the punishment of humanity but as the rebirth of human purpose rendered futile in the garden of Eden.

St. Theodore the Studite writes:

> How precious the gift of the cross, how splendid to contemplate! In the cross there is no mingling of good and evil as in the tree of paradise: it is wholly beautiful to behold and good to taste. The fruit of this tree is not death but life, not darkness but light. The tree does not cast us out of paradise, but opens the way for our return.[13]

Every one of us shares the tree of Christ's cross. Our sufferings are the doorway through which Christ shares his life with ours. Our sufferings too are the doorway through which Christ initiates and nourishes his friendship with us. We cannot experience heaven until we let our crosses "fill up what is lacking in the sufferings of Christ" (Col 1:24). The only thing Christ does not possess is our crosses. The good news is he wants them!

It must be said again and again that life's greatest consolation for people of faith is Christ's paschal mystery. This passover is a lifetime pilgrimage of carrying the cross of our inabilities so that we might be fully aware of heaven's presence within us. Those whose faith has given them the certainty of heaven's presence in the communion of saints do not need to describe it; their lives reveal it.

QUESTIONS FOR YOUR REFLECTION

1. In the Lord's Prayer we pray, "Thy kingdom come." If God's kingdom is already within us, why do we pray that it come?

2. What is the human limitation that sometimes creates the illusion of weak faith?

3. Why is our cross indispensable for faith's role to put us in touch with heaven's glory within us?

SATURDAY OF THE SECOND WEEK

Who Is Worthy to Open the Scroll?

WORD

> *"Worthy are you to receive the scroll*
> *and break open its seals,*
> *for you were slain"* (Rev. 5:9).

REFLECTION

One spring evening my father and I set out to plant several tomato plants. I found one with a broken stem. From my point of view, the little plant's utility had been replaced by futility.

My father saw the plant from another point of view. He carefully wrapped the broken stem and planted it deep in the soil. With a look of calm conviction he hummed a popular song, "Ah! Sweet Mystery of Life."

After the harvest I understood my father's point of view. The plant I had condemned outproduced the hardy ones a hundredfold. In time I realized that when my father hummed "Ah! Sweet Mystery of Life" he handed on to me a truth that said, "the brokenness of life is worthy of opening the scroll of life's mystery." I discovered that brokenness can be a credential for abundance. It did not escape my notice that the plant's brokenness opened it to the soil's healing. Hardy plants don't require healing.

When the author of Revelation was granted a vision of heaven, he saw a scroll no one could open except—ah! sweet mystery of life!—the "Lamb that had been slain" (Rev 5:6). There before the eyes of John stood one who "emptied himself . . . accepting even death, death on a cross!" (Phil 2:7-8). This Lamb, being born in the likeness of humankind" (see Phil 2:7), ascended into heaven bearing the marks of brokenness and healing. The Son of God gave to heaven the brokenness it had never possessed so that heaven might give to earth the healing it had lost.

Both heaven and earth recognize the worth of the Lamb to open the scroll as they sing:

> Worthy are you to receive the scroll
>> and break open its seals,
>> for you were slain.
>
> With your blood you purchased for God
>> men [and women] of every race and tongue,
>> of every people and nation.
>
> You made of them a kingdom,
>> and priests to serve our God,
>> and they shall reign on the earth (Rev 5:9-10).

Seen in this light, are we wise to toss aside the sufferings of our lives? Is suffering seen as no more than condemnation? How can we flee from that which Christ embraced as the indispensable instrument for healing? The door of heaven's healing is our brokenness, and through it we can see before us heaven's mystery of life.

Heaven's mystery of life is the paschal mystery. When Christ was slain, the door to life's hidden presence was opened by Christ's death and resurrection to become heaven's way to the imperishability of eternal life. Christ's brokenness shattered the myth that nothing is better than the "good life" of this world. Christ's resurrection became humankind's certainty that the sovereignty of this world's "good life" is a lie.

We can ill afford to toss aside our brokenness as I was so tempted to do with a small, broken tomato plant. Our brokenness is an instrument of salvation. It calls from God healings which strengths don't need. Heaven has not experienced the precise way each of us suffers. The paschal mystery is really Christ's Passover pilgrimage—from presence in our brokenness to presence in our healing. Christ will be our healing when we let him share our brokenness.

QUESTIONS FOR YOUR REFLECTION

1. Why did the serpent's lie close the door of life's mystery to Adam and Eve (see Gen 3:4-6)?

2. Why did Jesus' death on the cross qualify him to break the seals of humankind's mystery of life? What is the mystery of life Adam and Eve's disobedience sealed off from all of humanity?

3. Suffering is never easy or enjoyable. Why, then, is it imperative for salvation? In what way does our brokenness qualify us to discover— ah! life's sweet mystery?

4. In the light of the reflection, what did Jesus mean when he said "The healthy do not need a doctor; sick people do" (Luke 5:31)?

THIRD SUNDAY OF EASTER

Eucharist Leads to Justice

WORD

"The apostles, in their recollections, which are called gospels, handed down to us what Jesus commanded them to do. They tell us that he took bread, gave thanks and said: 'Do this in memory of me, "This is my body." In the same way he took the cup, he gave thanks and said, "This is my blood." ' . . . Ever since then we have constantly reminded one another of these things. The rich among us help the poor and we are always united" (St. Justin Martyr).[14]

REFLECTION

One hot summer day, a newly commissioned minister of the Eucharist brought Communion to an elderly invalid in her home. Taken aback by its abandoned appearance, with storm windows still fixed in place in the stifling heat and the yard's knee-high weeds, the Eucharistic minister decided that the premises needed attention.

After receiving Communion, the communicant lamented the death of an elderly neighbor who had formerly removed storm windows, cared for the lawn, and shopped for her groceries each week. Her eyes filled with tears and she sobbed, "I don't know where to turn."

It was the Feast of Corpus Christi, and as the minister of the sacrament listened to her plea he recalled a sentence from the pastor's homily: "Eucharist leads to justice!" There in the stifling heat of a helpless invalid's home, he murmured, "Amen!"

By five o'clock on that Feast of Corpus Christi, a father, mother, and their five children had restored the elderly woman's home to a state of livability. It was to this that the Eucharist had led them. It was for her peace of mind and comfort that the family had ministered the meaning of the Eucharist.

Eucharist begins on the altar, but its mission is to bring God's justice to the world. Both ministers and communicants of the Eucharist's sacramental presence become ministers of justice and peace beyond the altar's precincts when they see themselves as sacraments of justice and peace. The consistency between *what* sacraments signify and *how* that significance is translated into reality is the sign of living faith.

John, Revelation's author, sees the Lamb open seven seals. From three of them thunder forth the injustices of plunder, slaughter, and death. But from under the altar there emerges from the suffering martyrs a cry: "How long will it be, O Master, holy and true, before you judge our cause and avenge our blood among the inhabitants of the earth?" (Rev 6:10-11).

It must not go unnoticed that the cries of the martyrs come from "under the altar" (Rev 6:9). The Lamb who was slain and who was raised up had already heard the cries of the oppressed. Christ's Eucharistic presence signifies his readiness to be taken where there is injustice and its many forms of oppression. The Eucharistic presence of Jesus longs to accompany us as we carry his presence to be witnesses of his love for the poor.

The resurrection of Christ is a challenge to make the Eucharist a way of living. The risen Christ lives among us not to be confined to altars but to be communicated to the world. When Jesus said, "This is my body. . . . This is my blood" (Mark 14:22-23), he spoke not only of his sacramental presence but also of his *witnessed* presence among those whose presence is the dignity of being like God.

Jesus longed to be the nourishment of that dignity. "Do this as a remembrance of me" (Luke 22:19), he pleaded. As he shared his sacramental presence with the disciples, he commissioned them to share his presence in behalf of the poor and their human dignity. This is the basis for genuine Eucharistic devotion. A Eucharistic devotion which does not extend beyond its sanctuary precincts turns them into museums of piety away from the voices of Christ's companions in poverty as they cry: "How long will it be, O Master, holy and true, before you judge our cause and avenge our blood among the inhabitants of the earth?"

In *deed* Eucharist leads to justice where peace will be its fruit!

QUESTIONS FOR YOUR REFLECTION

1. In Christ's words "Do this in memory of me" what is "this"?

2. When people complain, "I don't get anything out of Mass," what do you think is the real reason they make that complaint?

3. In the Catholic Church, Sunday worship is an obligation. When that obligation is regarded as physical presence only, what aspect of the Eucharist is absent from one's larger and ennobling understanding of Eucharist?

4. Perhaps you have heard people say, "I am glad that the jury gave that man the justice he had coming!" How does this evidence of court justice differ from the justice to which the Eucharist beckons us?

MONDAY OF THE THIRD WEEK

Rain Man: Charlie's Great Trial

WORD

> *"Then one of the elders asked me, 'Who are these people all dressed in white? And where have they come from?' I said to him, 'Sir, you should know better than I.' He then told me, 'These are the ones who have survived the great period of trial; they have washed their robes and made them white in the blood of the Lamb"* (Rev 7:13-14).

REFLECTION

Rain Man is a surprising movie. Dustin Hoffman's accurate portrayal of autism's self-preoccupation surprises few. Supporting actor Tom Cruise's brilliant portrayal of one who is transformed by his autistic brother's "great period of trial" surprises us all.

Charlie Babbit and his brother, "Rain Man," travel by car from Ohio to California. On that long cross-country journey Charlie changes from an arrogant, angry, and aggressive money hustler to a caring, gentle, and compassionate brother. The trying ways of Rain Man's autism call forth from Charlie a treasury of goodness and beauty few moviegoers dream he possesses.

Rain Man has touched millions of lives because it touches a symbol which all understand. It symbolizes Sacred Scripture's Exodus story of a people who are transformed into a community of free people marked with the seal of salvation. That seal is the transformation of those who journey from fantasy to reality.

Each person's exodus story is one of trial. Step by step throughout our life's journey we face the demands of our ego to make fantasy the only reality of life. At every step of the way we are tempted to the autism that regards one's own view of reality as the whole of reality.

The exodus experience invites us to look beyond our own perceptions of reality for the connectedness that lifts us out of ourselves to make us whole. Human wholeness must include communion with God and one another. The exodus experience calls us out of ourselves to be transformed into the identity that embraces much more than our egomania.

Charlie's "great period of trial" with his autistic brother, Rain Man, forces him to face his own spiritual autism. He begins his journey with prospects of becoming three million dollars richer. At the end of his "trial" pilgrimage with his brother, the once-greedy Charlie couldn't care less about the prospect of being a millionaire. His newly discovered love for his brother removes the dollar signs from his eyes and frees him to see only his brother.

In a sense, Charlie Babbit is symbolic of Revelation's "huge crowd which no one could count from every nation and race, people and tongue" (Rev 7:9). This "huge crowd" are the Charlie Babbits, who step by step face and overcome autism's lie that all of this life revolves around their own perception of human purpose. Marked on their foreheads is the seal of Christ's own exodus experience. That mark is humanity's passover from preoccupation with self to the freedom of being servants of God.

At each step of our earthly pilgrimage we are graced to set free from the depths of ourselves the identity of beauty and goodness which we truly are. Who are we? We are "a chosen race, a royal priesthood, a holy nation, a people [God] claims for his own to proclaim the glorious works of the One who called [us] from darkness into his marvelous light" (1 Pet 2:9). We are called to give witness of transformation.

At the end of the long and ardous journey from Ohio, Charlie Babbit has been transformed to embrace the fullness of Rain Man's brotherhood. Rain Man's autism heals Charlie's. The brother Charlie had forgotten becomes the instrument of the healing Charlie little dreams he needs. Raymond's autism does not cease, but Charlie's does. Unwittingly perhaps, he becomes a servant of God in whose image and likeness he finds his real self. From the hiddenness of Charlie's many mansions overshadowed by his once-monstrous ego, there comes forth into the light of reality a truly beautiful, gracious, and caring brother.

In the light of Christ's Passover story, is the story of Rain Man really surprising?

QUESTIONS FOR YOUR REFLECTION

1. How does autism's failure to make connections relate to a failure to let faith make connections? In what way does faith make connections?

2. Give some examples from the New Testament of religious leaders' failures to make connections. In what way was the Law an instrument of disconnectedness in terms of these leaders failure to relate to Christ?

3. In what way can you connect the Old Testament's Exodus experience with your own passover experience of life?

Sing a New Song!

WORD

"It is your unquestioned desire to sing of him whom you love, but you ask me how to sing his praises. You have heard the words: 'Sing to the Lord a new song,' and you wish to know what praises to sing. The answer is: 'His praise is in the assembly of the saints'; it is in the singers themselves. If you desire to praise him, then live what you express. Live good lives and you yourselves will be his praise" (St. Augustine, bishop).[15]

REFLECTION

Not long after an abused and unloved child was welcomed into a loving home, his foster family gathered to celebrate the boy's birthday. The party was a new experience for the lad. When the family had finished their vigorous and vibrant rendition of "Happy Birthday to You," they invited the boy to blow out the candles on the cake. With a big smile on his face he replied, "I'd rather sing that new song!"

The psalms invite us to "Sing to the LORD a new song" (Ps 98:1). We are invited to sing because music, more than words, expresses our intimacy with God. When we are loved we simply cannot verbalize the transformation to which love leads us because we can't define its presence. Abba, Amen, Alleluia—what are these but sounds of the "new song" that God sings within the newness of our transformed hearts overcome with God's transcendent love?

The "new song" we are called to express is a way of living consistent with God's indwelling Word. St. Augustine speaks to his people of this consistency: "Yes, indeed, you are singing: you are singing clearly, I can hear you. But make sure that your life does not contradict your words. Sing with your voices, your hearts, and your lips, and your lives: 'Sing to the Lord a new song.' "[16]

The "new song" is life lived in harmony with God's presence. The "new song" is the wholeness—the holiness—of our being, where the harmony of our personhood reveals this world's dissonant sounds. With Christ at the center of our lives all other centerings are off key.

With Christ at the center of his life, St. Paul sings this "new song" in countless ways:

> I consider the sufferings of the present to be as nothing compared with the glory to be revealed in us (Rom 8:18).
>
> I have been crucified with Christ, and the life I live now is not my own; Christ is living in me (Gal 2:19-20).
>
> For, to me, "life" means Christ (Phil 1:21).
>
> I have accounted all else rubbish so that Christ may be my wealth and I may be in him, not having any justice of my own (Phil 3:8-9).

St. Paul's theme? Jesus Christ is at the core of human life. He declares all other centerings, including the Law, as "rubbish" in the light of the purpose for which God created humanity's personhood. Having encountered Christ, Paul sees that God's "Law" is the way, the truth, and the life of Jesus. Christ, he insists, is God's imperative, in whom humankind can justify its reason for being. Around Jesus, all human life has been harmonized and orchestrated. This wholeness of personhood is St. Paul's "new song" whose lyric is the risen Christ.

John, the author of Revelation, describes a poignant moment: "When the Lamb broke open the seventh seal, there was silence in heaven for about half an hour" (Rev 8:1). All of heaven becomes silent because its inhabitants listen with rapt attention as "the smoke of the incense went up before God, and with it the prayers of God's people" (Rev 8:4). Heaven's companions pause to listen because they feel a kinship with God's earthly companions. Heaven resonates with earth, and in a moment of silence both heaven and earth sing with their hearts "the new song" of their companionship.

The saints feel a kinship and a communion with all of those on earth when their lives are in union with the life of the risen Christ. This is the intimacy that guarantees the listening of heaven's audience when earth's companions gather at worship to sing "the new song" of Christ's risen presence. Heaven listens when earth's prayers rise like incense while humanity sings of its image and likeness of God.

A small boy sang when he discovered that he was loved. For the first time in his life, love made everything else seem as "rubbish." Nothing of his birthday party mattered except one thing: "I'd rather sing that new song!"

QUESTIONS FOR YOUR REFLECTION

1. When we can't verbalize the depths of an experience, why does music enable us to express it? Why did the little boy feel like singing?

2. In what way is a singing parish significant? What have the people discovered about Christ?

3. The Bible clearly states that God's creation is good. Is St. Paul, then, contradicting Sacred Scripture when he accounts everything outside of Christ as "rubbish"?

4. What is the reason for heaven's "silence"? What is the consistency that brings it about?

WEDNESDAY OF THE THIRD WEEK

Born Again?

WORD

"Our first birth took place without our knowledge or consent. . . . We needed a new birth of which we ourselves would be conscious, and which would be the result of our own free choice" (St. Justin Martyr).[17]

REFLECTION

St. John's Gospel offers us a picture of a greatly disturbed man. Nicodemus is torn between his Pharisaic dedication to the Law and his attraction to Jesus of Nazareth. His late-hour visit to Jesus is evidence of his deep desire to bridge the goodness of the Law with his perception of Jesus as a man of God.

"Rabbi," he begins, "we know you are a teacher come from God, for no man can perform signs and wonders such as you perform unless God is with him" (John 3:2). It becomes apparent, as we read between these lines, that Nicodemus cries out to Jesus for help to resolve his dilemma. Jesus replies:

"I solemnly assure you,
no one can see the reign of God
unless he is begotten from above" (John 3:3).

Begotten from above? The dilemma widens for Nicodemus. He is astonished: "How can a man be born again once he is old?" (John 3:4).

Nicodemus hears Christ's words with a literalness that threatens his birth to transcendence from the womb of faith which Christ longs for him to share. For him, birth means only the emergence of life from the mother's womb. In this moment of the Pharisee's "spiritual autism" Christ endeavors to raise his mind and heart to be touched by God's Holy Spirit. Christ invites his troubled night visitor to follow faith's lead beyond what we know and what we have seen (see John 3:11) to the knowing and seeing begotten of God's Spirit. "Spirit begets spirit" (John 3:6), Jesus replies.

Here was the center of Christ's encounter with Nicodemus: He challenged him to believe that God created human life for a destiny beyond this world's boundaries. Jesus invited him to embrace the truth that God's Spirit has come for the rebirth of humankind's fullest destiny. Christ wanted Nicodemus to see with the eyes of faith that from our mothers' wombs we enter a world that in itself provides no resource for humankind's embrace of eternal life. But in the womb of this world's pilgrimage toward human destiny, Christ insisted, God's Spirit is heaven's resource for begetting our inheritance of eternal life. This inheritance is why God created humankind.

Jesus' encounter with Nicodemus is also ours. All of us are called to be born again into the womb of God's Spirit. And in this world, the awareness of human destiny is awakened, so that our free will can *choose* the destiny which God's Spirit longs to beget in the depths of our unlimited capacity to grow in God's likeness. This is the choice that makes possible our spirit's graced decision to be reborn and relinked with the destiny our first parents freely rejected in the Garden of Eden.

Jesus offered Nicodemus the good news that in this world the choice of God's kingdom is not beyond our reach. Indeed, heaven has come into our midst to be the destiny of all who, in the waters of baptism, open themselves to heaven's sacred presence. These life-giving waters offer us the choice of beginning dying's painful journey away from the illusion of this world to the rebirth of companionship with God's trinitarian life forever. St. Paul exclaims:

If we have died with Christ, we believe that we are also to live with him. We know that Christ, once raised from the dead, will never die again; death has no more power over him. His death was death to sin, once for all; his life is life for God. In the same way, you must consider yourselves dead to sin but alive for God in Christ Jesus (Rom 6:8-11).

QUESTIONS FOR YOUR REFLECTION

1. A wide chasm between Nicodemus' fidelity to the Law and his wonder about Jesus had kept them apart. What bridge did Jesus endeavor to erect in order to close the chasm?

2. We do not choose human life, yet it is necessary for us to choose eternal life. Why?

3. Martyrs are those who witness their faith by dying for it. In what way is martyrdom the sign that they have chosen to be born again into eternal life?

4. Today, abortion and euthanasia are promoted in the name of the "sanctity of human choice." In what way have pro-abortionists and pro-euthanasiaists deformed the dignity of free choice? If human choice possesses the "sanctity" that justifies its decision to take life, how can that decision be born of the Spirit?

THURSDAY OF THE THIRD WEEK

The Makers of Idols Become Them

WORD

"That part of mankind which escaped the plagues did not repent of the idols they had made. They did not give up the worship of demons, or of gods made from gold and silver, from bronze and stone and wood, which cannot see or hear or walk" (Rev 9:20).

REFLECTION

These words of Revelation echo those of the psalmist:

> [The] idols [of pagans] are silver and gold,
>> the handiwork of men.
> They have mouths but speak not;
>> they have eyes but see not;
> They have ears but hear not;
>> they have noses but smell not;
> They have hands but feel not;
>> they have feet but walk not;
>> they utter no sound from their throat (Ps 115:4-7).

The psalmist draws this picture of idols in order to establish a frightening truth:

> Their makers shall be like them,
>> everyone that trusts in them (Ps 115:8).

The alarming aspect of idolatry lies not in the makeup of the idols but in our created capacity to trust them, worship them, and become them. It is ironic that our radical difference from all other creation is the very factor that can reduce us to creation's peership. God created our creaturehood to share creatorship, not usurp it. How tragic that our creaturehood can be reduced to the indignity of sharing peership with creaturehood's likeness to lesser creatures!

What is idolatry? It is the establishing of that which is perishable at the center of our lives. While these centerpieces are not evil in themselves, the fact that they become the center of our lives opens the door for the evil of our *becoming what we have enthroned there.*

Our becoming what we make central raises the issue of salvation. At the center of salvation's meaning is the belonging that gives us identity:

> Their makers [of idols] shall be like them,
>> everyone that trusts in them.

We need to understand that belonging and identity are inescapably related. We are by nature social because we have been created to share the identity of God. This identity *must* be at the center of our lives because our belonging to God is our reason for existence. To have that belonging, with the inestimable identity to which it is related, is the meaning of salvation.

If any creaturehood becomes the centerpiece of our lives, its inescapable belonging will not be "of God." St. John reminds us that "flesh begets flesh" (John 3:6). Whatever of this world we enthrone at the center of our human purpose "begets" persishability. For that reason, salvation is imperiled because God created us to be imperishable.

It is interesting that Christ offered us the perishability of bread and wine as the sign of his presence at the center of our lives. The Church clearly teaches that bread and wine become the "good gift" of Christ's identity. This Eucharistic celebration of a lesser creaturehood's belonging, its very identity with Christ, calls us to reexamine the radiant dignity of God's human creation. Christ's Eucharistic presence in the perishability of bread and wine cries out for the understanding of his longing to be clothed in the perishability of our humanity so that it might be raised to God's imperishability.

"How can it be said," St. Irenaeus asks, "that flesh belonging to the Lord's own body and nourished by his body and blood is incapable of receiving God's gift of eternal life?"[18] The Eucharist is the sacrament of Christ's call for us to place his presence at the center of our lives. This is the centrality that Christ longs for us to enthrone so that he might give worship to God clothed in our earthly existence. When we have become the imperishability we were created to become, we live in this world as sacraments of salvation.

QUESTIONS FOR YOUR REFLECTION

1. Addiction arises from the placing of something other than God at the center of our lives. How does this relate to the psalmist's words, the "makers [of idols] shall be like them, everyone that trusts in them"?

2. Our ideal receives most of our thinking, most of our conversation, and most of our money. In the light of this, what is your ideal? Is it perishable or imperishable?

3. How are belonging and identity "inescapably related"?

4. How does the Eucharist dignify inanimate creation? How would you explain that the centering of bread and wine as Christ's sacramental presence is not the practice of idolatry?

Is Death a Failure?

WORD

"I took the little scroll from the angel's hand and ate it. In my mouth it tasted as sweet as honey, but when I swallowed it my stomach turned sour" (Rev 10:10).

REFLECTION

Death is not the failure of human existence. Death is the failure of this world's claim to possess the capacity of satisfying humanity's longing for the sweetness of God's presence. That claim is a lie. The illusion of eternal sweetness from the fruit of this world's perishability became Adam and Eve's choice of a perishable destiny. In that lie lurked death's "sting."

To Mary, humankind's "second Eve," God offered the truth of humanity's imperishable destiny. God's Word was the Truth she was asked to receive into her womb. Mary, who was asked to eat of heaven's "scroll," tasted the sweetness of Christ's conception within her womb. With that sweetness, she was to taste the bitter implications of Christ's presence from those who saw the implications of his earthly mission.

Death is not a final failure. Life's final failure is the acceptance of the "sting" that the fruits of this world's sweetness are at the center of humanity's existence. Death is not the end; death is birth! Our daily dyings are but the birth pangs of the eternal life that God's presence longs to unfold within us:

> The sadness of death gives way
> to the bright promise of immortality.
> Lord, for your faithful people life is changed, not ended.
> When the body of our earthly dwelling lies in death,
> we gain an everlasting dwelling place in heaven.[19]

St. Paul taunts death when he asks, "O death, where is your victory? O death, where is your sting?" (1 Cor 15:55). Death's victory lies not in its power to end life but in its capacity to unveil the illusion of this world's claim of everlasting sweetness. The resurrection of Jesus from death's "sting" became the "sting" that ended death's bid to be humanity's failure.

"O death, where is your victory?" St. Paul calls us to confront the irony that humanity's perishability becomes the *instrument* of its imperishability. Jesus' humanity is the key. When Jesus was raised from the dead all of human life was raised to be reowned to the imperishability of God's identity, which human life was created to share forever. St. Ephrem writes: "Death slew [Jesus] by means of his body which he had assumed, but that same body proved to be the weapon with which he conquered death."[20]

The frame of reference within which we tend to discern human life's meaning is the erroneous belief that meeting this world's criteria for success is the way to measure meaning. Tragic as this is, it is even more tragic to believe that our lives have been failures because we have been duped by death's "sting." Our failures are wonderful opportunities to move into that frame of reference we call faith. Faith frees us from the tenuous moorings of this world's illusions of glory. In the world of faith we are secured to the moorings of the divine identity which all of us have been created to share for all eternity.

It is never easy to depart from this world's moorings. But the "victory" of death is our opportunity to move with faith into the unfamiliar realms of God's presence. The victory of our departure from this life's moorings lies in our faithfulness to God's call to enter God's way of truth and life. This way invites us to die to the world's criteria of measuring success. Faith takes us to the mooring that lies beyond this world's claims of security, to the "sting" that robs death of its power to dupe. To believe that each departure from its mooring of perishability toward God's vision of imperishability makes all previous moorings not worth nostalgia's bid for their return.

Anthony de Mello, S.J., offers this story:

> A man came upon a tall tower and stepped inside to find it all dark. As he groped around, he came upon a circular staircase. Curious to know where it led to, he began to climb, and as he climbed, he sensed a growing uneasiness in his heart. So he looked behind him and was horrified to see that each time he climbed a step, the previous one fell off and disappeared. Before him the stairs went upward and he had no idea where they led; behind him yawned an enormous black emptiness.[21]

God's Word tastes sweet when it calls us to step up; fear, however, may tempt us when we realize that we can't go back.

QUESTIONS FOR YOUR REFLECTION

1. Mother Teresa of Calcutta was once accused of being a failure for treating the terminally ill rather than the curably sick. She answered, "God never asks us to be successful; God only asks that we be faithful." What are your thoughts about her reply?

2. What is the sinfulness that leads us to accept death as life's failure? In what sense is death a birth?

3. How does faith enable death to be a "victory" over death?

4. What would you say is the radical difference between the crucified Christ's good news about death and the world's gospel about death?

SATURDAY OF THE THIRD WEEK

God's Measuring Rod

WORD

"Someone gave me a measuring rod and said: 'Come and take the measurements of God's temple and altar, and count those who worship there. Exclude the outer court of the temple, however; do not measure it, for it has been handed over to the Gentiles, who will crush the holy city for forty-two months. I will commission my two witnesses to prophesy for those twelve hundred and sixty days, dressed in sackcloth' " (Rev 11:1-3).

REFLECTION

When the contemporaries of Johann Sebastian Bach heard his music, they scorned and ridiculed it. Bach's music was rejected because his listeners measured it by music familiar to their ears. That all of this has changed is the evidence that contemporary classical music is measured by Bach's.

To measure the new by the old is unavoidable. It becomes a danger, however, when the attitude "we've never done it that way before" becomes our only measure of worth. This is especially true of the criteria which human worth requires in terms of a dignity the world cannot bestow. God is the criterion of human dignity, and it is from God that human dignity can be measured. How, then, does God measure the worth of human identity?

John is asked to measure the altar and the Temple and to count those who gather to worship there. He is commanded to exclude all who gather in the Temple's outer court. In that area he sees the Gentiles, witnesses of this world's ways of measuring human worth. The Gentiles, John notes, "will crush the holy city for forty-two months." But he quickly adds a ray of hope: "I will commission my two witnesses to prophesy for those twelve hundred and sixty days, . . ."

The images of altar, Temple, and witness emphasize the necessity of measuring human dignity by its purpose and worth. Those who offer measurements based only on this world's values in the "outer court" of God's sovereignty measure with instruments hardly adequate to esteem the identity God has created humankind to share. When altar, Temple, and witness are not considered as measurements integral to human dignity, some lesser measure of worth will always become the centerpiece of human existence.

The "altar" stands as the measure of our willingness to be witnesses of sacrifice. Sunday after Sunday the altar challenges us to the wholeness of human purpose, which of necessity demands the pain of releasing ourselves from any "outer court" measurements of human dignity. God never ceases to call us to the oneness that characterizes God's identity. It is never easy to respond to the imperative of living in the likeness of God's trinitarian life. Nevertheless, this imperative is the essence of the sacrifice necessary for becoming identified with God. To have another centerpiece of life is evidence of the brokenness that betrays our human worth in the eyes of God.

We gather around the altar as God's "temple" because *we* are the church, assembling each Sunday to rededicate ourselves to the sacrificial life of Christ as the center of our existence. This gathering is our unceasing response to the vocation of building the church. The church is never finished because we who are in the likeness of God are never finished growing in Christ. It is by way of our unique giftedness that the church continues to be built.

We, the "temple" of God—the church—gather as witnesses of God's identity never before seen in the church. Our witness of sacrifice gives birth, again and again, to a human worth not recognized in this world's "outer court" of perishable values. Our sacrificial witness paves the way for the Spirit's witness of God's trinitarian identity in the precincts of God's "temple."

Jesus was sent by God to be "altar," "temple," and "witness." He was sent into the "outer court" of human existence where all of reality had been measured by the instruments of this world's vision of "salvation." Jesus Christ was scorned, ridiculed, and condemned for being this world's unfamiliar criterion for salvation. Christ's "way" did not measure up to the world's "way" of self-indulgence. He paid the price of being God's "temple" and God's "witness" by suffering the sacrifice of his life on the "altar" of the cross.

It was upon this "altar" that God unlocked the heavens and poured the fullness of glory into this world's "outer court" of emptiness. The Father revealed that glory when he raised Jesus from the dead. Christ's resurrection, the fruit of his sacrifice, became the measure of God's love for humanity, his temple here on earth. Our lives of sacrifice become the witness of the measure with which we value God.

QUESTIONS FOR YOUR REFLECTION

1. Why is God's gift of faith necessary to be in touch with heaven's ways of measuring human purpose?

2. Why is it true that when we try to compare God's measure of human purpose with the things of this world, our comparisons limp?

3. It has been said that "we've never done it that way before" are the seven last words. In what sense does the refusal to lead sacrificial lives give truth to this statement? Basically, what is *the* sacrifice God asks of us?

4. In the light of this chapter's reflection, what is your reflection concerning the obligation to gather weekly around the altar of Eucharistic celebration? How does that weekly gathering build the church?

Revelation: The Bible's Cold Book?

WORD

> *"A great sign appeared in the sky, a woman clothed with the sun, with the moon under her feet, and on her head a crown of twelve stars"* (Rev 12:1).

REFLECTION

The appearance of coldness in the Book of Revelation relates more to our unfamiliarity with its symbolism than to the hidden meaning it contains. When, however, we manage to penetrate the mystery of its symbols, we find its warmth.

The hiddenness of Revelation's warmth emerges in its twelfth chapter. We are beckoned to discover the author's own deep compassion and sensitivity to the the many Christians whose discipleship led them into a land of suffering. John's compassion calls him to enter this land with words of hope that have enabled Christ's followers to see suffering as "a great sign . . . in the sky, a woman clothed with the sun." This woman who was the symbol of these sufferings was with child, a child who was destined to be their joy and their peace.

John invites his readers to believe that their trials are not without meaning. He holds out to them the warmth of God's Word, leading them into the deep recesses of spiritual maternity where the warmth of God's risen Son can be found. John writes, "Because she was with child, she wailed aloud in pain as she labored to give birth" (Rev 12:2).

Within the context of the Church's liturgical expression of Revelation, the "great sign . . . a woman clothed with the sun" has been variously identified as the Virgin Mary, the Church, Israel, and Jerusalem. These identities cannot be lightly dismissed. In every respect they do relate to John's meaning of "woman" in the Book of Revelation.

The issue, however, of who the woman is ought not negate the issue of what the "woman" means. To go beyond the woman's identity to "woman" as humankind's destiny is the issue Adela Yarbro Collins raises: "The interpretation of chapter 12 . . . does not try to identify the woman clothed with the sun as many interpretations do. . . . Her importance for the Apocalypse lies not so much in her identity as in her destiny. . . . [The 'woman'] should be seen as a story which interprets the first readers' experience."[22]

It goes without saying that this story should also be interpreted in the light of *our* destiny. Those who follow Christ are called to a destiny beyond this world's limits. That destiny is not without suffering because deep within the hiddenness of our identity lies our destiny to be united to Christ crucified, waiting to be raised up through us, with us, and in us. In our destiny of sufferings here on earth there is also the certainty that the fruits of God's joy and peace are our destiny for all eternity.

The Easter season is a time of joy. But it is also a time of remembering that joy is delivered from the womb of suffering. The symbolism of humanity's maternal agonies must first be accepted before we can fully embrace the fruit of humanity's maternal joy, Christ's risen presence in our lives. Our sufferings are the longings of Christ, waiting to be raised up in our time so that his "time" of never-ending resurrection might break forth like the dawn.

Concluding a beautiful Easter homily, St. Gregory the Great exhorts:

> Let us set out for [eternal life] where we shall keep joyful festival with so many of our fellow citizens. May the thought of their happiness urge us on! Let us stir up our hearts, rekindle our faith, and long eagerly for what heaven has in store for us. To love thus is to be already on our way. No matter what the obstacles we encounter, we must not allow them to turn us aside from the joy of that heavenly feast. Anyone who is determined to reach his destination is not deterred by the roughness of the road that leads to it.[23]

QUESTIONS FOR YOUR REFLECTION

1. In terms of one's sufferings, how does Revelation's twelfth chapter offer words of warmth and compassion? What is the specific reason why our sharing in Christ's resurrection must be accompanied by suffering?

2. Without discarding the Church's imagery of Mary as "the great sign . . . in the sky," what other meaning of that image offers us the means to share Christ's risen presence in our lives?

3. How does Revelation's author transform the sufferings of this world into sources of warmth and joy?

4. How does John's woman-child image reveal to you Easter's Passover mystery?

MONDAY OF THE FOURTH WEEK

Water Is Both Death and Life

WORD

"There is in baptism an image both of death and life, the water being the symbol of death, the Spirit giving the pledge of life" (St. Basil the Great, bishop).[24]

REFLECTION

June 10, 1970, is indelibly imprinted on my memory. On that late spring day a fellow priest, Fr. Jim Rasmussen, drowned in the waters of a sand pit near a retreat house. He died trying to save the life of a stranger.

The tragedy happened, ironically, after the priest and two companions had decided that the water was too cold for swimming. As they dozed in the sun's warmth, which they had traded for the water's chill, a man's cry from the icy waters called for help. Father Rasmussen, an expert swimmer, responded immediately. As he encountered the thrashings of the terror-stricken man, it became obvious that the priest's swimming expertise was no match for the drowning man's lock of death around his neck. Both of them drowned.

My friend's death plunged me into the waters of grief. But from that grief, the witness of his heroic love has magnified my awareness of baptism's meaning. My friend's consent to surrender his life for another's has challenged me to consent to a way of living consistent with the love that enables us to be magnifiers of baptism's sacramental significance. Father Rasmussen consented to risk his life in order to save another's. His witness has invited me to believe more sincerely that the vocation of baptism invites our consent to love God as Christ has loved us.

Baptism is the vocation of consenting both to death and to life. We are called to live Christ's way of life, sealed on our lives by the sacrament of baptism. Christ's way is the lived significance of baptism's death-resurrection meaning. His life is evidence that the perishability of the world's way is not humankind's final destiny. We are called to drown that perishability in the waters of baptism.

But baptism also calls us to a reality we cannot see with our eyes. Its waters invite us to see with the eyes of faith the imperishability of eternal life, which God has created us to *be*. Like a never-ending fountain of water in which we shall never again know thirst, God's imperishability becomes baptism's living reality. Jesus says:

> "Whoever drinks the water I give him
> will never be thirsty;
> no, the water I give
> shall become a fountain within him,
> leaping up to provide eternal life" (John 4:14).

Deep within the death-dealing waters of baptism there also dwells the life-giving waters of God's Spirit. In a very real sense, Father Rasmussen gave visible evidence of the Spirit's presence to which his lifesaving instincts called him to respond. The cry of a drowning man was heard in the rescuer's spirit-filled heart as he ignored his own cautions about the dangers lurking in the cold waters of the sand pit. The spirit-filled fountain of God's love sent him forth with life-giving intent.

The story of this priest's death offers us a deeper appreciation of baptism's vocation to pass over from this world's illusions of promise to God's promise of eternal enlightenment. Hidden within the waters of our baptism is the vocation of dying daily to our preoccupation with self. As a small child said, "Sin is sin because 'I' is in the middle of it."

Father Rasmussen's response to a cry for help challenges our faith to reach out beyond our "I" to see the needs of others in remembrance of Christ's witness to God's image and likeness. His saving efforts call us to renew our dedication to baptism's lived significance. Our baptismal renewal will bear fruit in our witness of the love that is God's identity. Baptism's significance, which calls all of us to be mirrors of God's love, moves St. Basil the Great to write:

> Through the Holy Spirit we are restored to paradise, we ascend
> to the kingdom of heaven, and we are reinstated as adopted
> [children]. Thanks to the Spirit we obtain the right to call God our

Father, we become sharers in the grace of Christ, we are called children of the light, and we share in everlasting glory. In a word, every blessing is showered upon us, both in this world and in the world to come. As we contemplate them even now, like a reflection in a mirror, it is as though we already possessed the good things our faith tells us that we shall one day enjoy. If this is the pledge, what will the perfection be? If these are the firstfruits, what will the full harvest be?[25]

QUESTIONS FOR YOUR REFLECTION

1. In what way does grief enable us to pass over from bitterness to peace in the face of the loss of people whose lives we cherish?
2. Why is the sacrament of baptism celebrated only once? In what way is its significance renewed again and again?
3. What do the words "born again" mean in the light of baptism's passover mystery? How is "born again" a continuous experience?
4. What person in your life has been of baptismal significance for you? In what way has that person enabled you to pass over from one reality to another?

TUESDAY OF THE FOURTH WEEK

Fear: Not Beast but Beauty

WORD

"Honor God and give him glory, for his time has come to sit in judgment. Worship the Creator of heaven and earth, the Creator of the sea and the springs" (Rev 14:7).

REFLECTION

"The only thing we have to fear is fear itself." With these words, Franklin Delano Roosevelt began his presidency of the United States in 1933. He electrified the people of this nation with a courage that snatched them from the depths of depression. He inspired them to reach out again for a destiny they once believed to be their national identity. President Roosevelt challenged this nation to transform fear's beast into fear's beauty.

Fear's beast is terror. We fear with terror when we lack the wisdom that enlightens purpose. Without wisdom, we are left only with fear's beast. Terror's absence of the beauty that fear possesses can lead us to despair. When we no longer know what we fear and why we fear, then our loss of wisdom makes room for fear's beast to dethrone fear's beauty from the center of our lives.

Fear's beauty is wisdom. This gift of God's Spirit does not deny the presence of fear's beast lurking in the outer courts. Wisdom rests on the foundation of faith, which makes secure our quest for purpose eager to encounter the only fear "we have to fear."

Fear's beauty is the wisdom to stand in reverential awe of a human purpose that nothing can destroy. This purpose is not of our making, nor do we possess it only by a thread. Human purpose is of God's making, entitling us to the everlasting beauty of God's imperishable image and likeness. God's gift of wisdom, fear's beauty, allows us to embrace God's imperishability as our destiny.

Beasts and beauties fill the pages of Revelation's imagery. But standing far above them is the Lamb of God, the personhood of God's wisdom. John sees gathered before the Lamb the communion of "the hundred and forty-four thousand":

> Then the Lamb appeared in my vision. He was standing on Mount Zion, and with him were the hundred and forty-four thousand who had his name and the name of his Father written on their foreheads. . . . They were singing a new hymn before the throne, . . . This hymn no one could learn except the hundred and forty-four thousand who had been ransomed from the world (Rev 14:1, 3).

Who are those who stand with the Lamb and sing the new hymn no one can learn? They are those whose fear of God, marked with the beauty of wisdom, sing of an existence known only to them. No longer are they afraid that the loss of this world's perishables is the loss of their identity. Their fear is reverential as it stands with the Lamb of God in eternal intimacy, marked with the imperishability of God's identity.

Wisdom also enables us to embrace the communion of those whose number, one hundred and forty-four thousand, symbolizes the totality of God's intent for *all* of humankind. Wisdom's reverential fear leads to the joy of belonging to God's family. This wisdom is the beauty of our humanity, which God created to be the beauty of God. St. Peter Chrysologus asserts: "Listen to the Lord's appeal: I want you to see your own body, your members, your heart, your bones, your blood. You may fear what is divine, but why not love what is human? . . . Do not be afraid."[26]

What is the sign—the "seal"—which indicates that fear's beauty is alive and active in our lives? St. Paul opens the door to that question when he pleads, "I beg you through the mercy of God to offer your bodies as a living sacrifice holy and acceptable to God" (Rom 12:1). This sacrifice is not a barter born of terror. It is not the charade of "giving up" this world's possessions as collateral for the possession of a place among the "hundred and forty-four thousand." Rather, it is the sacrifice of letting go of this world's spirit in order that our wholeness, intimacy, and communion with God's trinitarian presence might become our identity.

St. Peter Chrysologus challenges his listeners: "Let your heart be an altar. Then with full confidence in God, present your body for sacrifice. God desires not death, but faith; God thirsts not for blood, but for self-surrender; God is not appeased by slaughter, but by the offering of your free will."[27]

QUESTIONS FOR YOUR REFLECTION

1. How would you explain that a "fear" of those you love is not a contradiction?

2. Someone has observed that the epitome of love is to help others see beauty in themselves. What is the "beast" that prevents us from showing that kind of love? Likewise, why do those we love often fear to respond when we try to help them see their beauty?

3. Why is it futile to fear exclusion from the "hundred and forty-four thousand"?

4. What is the sacrifice we are called to offer on the "altar" of our hearts?

Christ's Last Will and Testament

WORD

> *"In the sacrament of his body, [Christ] actually gives us his own flesh, which he has united to his divinity. This is why we are one, because the Father is in Christ and Christ is in us. He is in us through his flesh and we are in him. With him we form a unity which is in God"* (St. Hilary, bishop).[28]

REFLECTION

Jesus died leaving no earthly possessions. His nakedness on the cross remains as the sacrament of his poverty. But Jesus died leaving one possession he knew to be of God's image and within humankind's capacity to become. He willed

"that all may be one
as you, Father, are in me, and I in you;
I pray that they may be [one] in us,
that the world may believe that you sent me" (John 17:21).

With this prayer Jesus summarized his mission. He spoke simply but cogently about his life's meaning and its transforming purpose for human existence. His will was perfectly consistent with God's identity. God created us to be one as Father, Son, and Holy Spirit are one.

When God spoke to Moses from the burning bush, "I am who am" (Exod 3:14), the whole world heard God's name and humanity's reason for existence. Jesus came to reveal that God's "I Am" was his own oneness with God's trinity of persons. This oneness with God's "I Am" also became the justifying reason for all of humankind's existence. God's "I Am" justified our right to say "I am."

Our oneness with God and with one another is the Bible's meaning of "justice." Our identity and our existence are justified because of the oneness and communion we share with heaven and earth. All other reasons which the world asserts as justification for humanity's "I am" beget only illusion. Those who fall for this deceit become one with its fruits of isolation, loneliness, and poor self-esteem.

The Fathers of the Second Vatican Council offer a ringing affirmation of humanity's justification for existence:

> Just as God did not create men [and women] to live as individuals but to come together in the formation of social unity, so he willed to make [them] holy and save them, not as individuals without bond or link between them, but rather to make them into a people who might acknowledge him and serve him in holiness.[29]

Before anyone's last will and testament can be carried out, there is required visible, tangible evidence. In courts of justice a written and signed document signifies the spoken wishes of the deceased. Jesus left no such written document. But he did leave us his Church. Christ left his ecclesial Word to be the instrument and witness of God's oneness until the end of time. Christ founded the Church to reflect the oneness that convinces the world of his mission:

> "I pray that they may be [one] in us,
> that the world may believe that you sent me."

The justice of human existence, then, is reflected in the Church. God created humankind to be like God's trinitarian oneness. Jesus' union with both God and humanity is a living witness and testament of his communion with God. His last will and testament is the Church, whose human and graced bondedness among the baptized is its claim to be the identity of Jesus. Our celebration of the Eucharist is the remembering of our bondedness with God and the nobility of our communion with those who celebrate the Eucharist.

"In the sacrament of his body, [Christ] actually gives us his own flesh, which he has united to his divinity. This is why we are one, because the Father is in Christ and Christ is in us. He is in us through his flesh and we are in him. With him we form a unity which is in God."

QUESTIONS FOR YOUR REFLECTION

1. What proof of ecclesial identity verifies the authenticity of Jesus' mission here upon earth? According to Christ, what identifies the true Church?

2. What is the connection between the assertion of Vatican II that "God . . . willed to make men [and women] holy" and Christ's last will

and testament "that all may be one"? How are holiness and oneness—clearly witnessed by the Church—evidence that Christ's last will and testament has been "probated"?

3. Why is division among Christians the scandal of scandals? In the light of Christ's last will and testament, can this division be justified?

4. In what way is the Eucharist the sacrament of nobility? Is that nobility the reason we are obligated to celebrate it?

THURSDAY OF THE FOURTH WEEK

Taste It Yourself!

WORD

"Then I heard the altar cry out:

'Yes, Lord God Almighty,
your judgments are true and just!' "* (Rev 16:7).

REFLECTION

A little girl received her first taste of kiwi fruit. After a bite, her mother asked, "What does it taste like?" Falteringly she replied, "Its like . . . its . . . like . . . lets see, its like . . . " Unable to provide a suitable comparison, she pointed to the fruit and said, "Oh heck, Mom, why don't you taste it yourself!"

Not everything can be accurately described. For example, what analogy could be used to describe aliveness to the unborn? Our reply would have to be that of the little girl: "Taste it yourself!"

To describe life one needs to experience God as he is most precisely defined by St. John the Evangelist: "God is love" (1 John 4:16). From this definition, it follows that who God is, namely love, is the love that enables us to know what God is like. To love as God loves is to experience what it means to be alive.

To love as God loves is to taste life. God created us to share in the image and likeness of love and, therefore, to live love as the definition of our lives. This was the core of Jesus' message. His coming became heaven's analogy of what it means to be alive. He came to be faith's prism by which we are able to "taste and see how good the LORD is" (Ps 34:9). To taste the Lord is to love as God loves us.

> He who abides in love
> abides in God,
> and God in him (1 John 4:16).

On one occasion, a scribe asked Jesus which of the many commandments of the Law was the greatest. Jesus' response did not begin with commandments as humanity's way of living for God. Jesus began with God: "Hear, O Israel! The Lord our God is Lord alone!" (Mark 12:29).

Christ made clear that life's way to God is not by way of the Law but by way of the God of the living. Delicately Jesus drew the scribe away from his identity with commandments to his identity with the One who is the source of commandments. Jesus could offer no other imperative, no priority of commandments, save that of loving like God loves.

> "Therefore you shall love the Lord your God
> with all your heart,
> with all your soul,
> with all your mind,
> and with all your strength" (Mark 12:30).

But what earthly analogy could describe the totality of loving God as humankind's most important commandment? Jesus found only one:

> "This is the second,
> 'You shall love your neighbor as yourself' " (Mark 12:31).

"As yourself"? Yes, Jesus offered as prism for God's way of loving the love and care we give ourselves. He wanted the scribe to understand that loving God and neighbor like the love people are eager to show themselves is the fulfillment of all the commandments. Without this fullness of love for God and neighbor as the centerpiece of human existence, there is absolutely no sense of what it means to be alive.

God's judgment is not by way of commandment keeping but by way of our keeping God's Word. The Eucharist makes this assertion possible. God judges human life by the Eucharistic significance of its appearances of bread and wine dissolving within us. This dissolution signifies the totality of self which Christ witnessed on the cross and calls us to witness in the world. St. Paul writes: "I have been crucified with Christ, and the life I live now is not my own; Christ is living in me" (Gal 2:19-20).

When we receive Christ's presence under the appearances of bread and wine, we are called to "taste and see" the indissoluble love and aliveness of God all around us in those who hunger and thirst for it. We are challenged at each Eucharist to "Go in peace to love and serve the Lord." In no other way will we be able to answer what it means to be alive except to taste the Eucharist's lived significance on the sacrificial altar of our daily lives.

QUESTIONS FOR YOUR REFLECTION

1. When Jesus said, "The Lord our God is Lord alone," he warned against having other gods at the center of our lives. In what way did the religious leaders of his time make commandment keeping a god?

2. What is the difference between love of self and self-indulgence?

3. In what respect is Jesus himself a "new commandment"?

4. At what point in our lives are we most alive?

FRIDAY OF THE FOURTH WEEK

Humanity: The Mirror of Salvation

WORD

"Beloved, Jesus Christ is our salvation. . . . Through him our gaze penetrates the heights of heaven and we see, as in a mirror, the most holy face of God. Through Christ the eyes of our hearts are opened, and our weak and clouded misunderstanding reaches up toward the light" (St. Clement, pope).[30]

REFLECTION

A barefoot boy stepped on a jagged piece of mirror which cut his foot severely. Many stitches were required. He had not seen the broken mirror because the dirt that covered it had given it the dirt's likeness. The boy suffered harm because the mirror had become the lie which rendered impossible its mission to reflect.

This true story is a parable that reminds us of Christ's saving role in restoring humanity to its dignity. Jesus raised our flesh to the dignity of mirroring God's saving presence here upon earth. Through Christ's humanity "our gaze penetrates the heights of heaven and we see, as in a mirror, the most holy face of God."

Christ's humanity is our salvation because it is our creaturehood's way of touching all of reality—both human and divine. None of God's mercy and generosity could have been received by us except through the prism of human mediation. Humanity's belonging to Christ's divine identity enabled it to become the mirror, the prism, by which "the eyes of our hearts [might be] opened" to "the most holy face of God."

A spirituality which demands that we bypass our humanity to touch God is harmful because it is filled with promises that miss the mark of salvation. The heresy of Jansenism, for example, would have us believe that nothing human is good, beautiful, or true. This perversion of Christ's mission ignores his words "Whoever looks on me is seeing him who sent me" (John 12:45). It ignores the simple truth that Jesus gave to humanity his identity and through it revealed God to all of humankind. Jesus saw no possibility of his companions accepting his divinity except by way of their humanity.

A "spirituality" that seeks the mission of becoming like this world also becomes harmful. It is harmful because without the capacity of mirroring God's glory, humanity's perishability poses for the imperishability of human dignity. When humanity has no other appearance but that of this world, its failure to mirror heaven's imperishability bears the fruit of futility.

When we look into the mirror of humanity's Christened identity we see a mission that calls us to be the instrument by which God reowns all of humanity in a oneness that *is* the very image and likeness of God. Pope John Paul II writes: "Redemption gives back to God the work of creation which has been contaminated by sin, showing the perfection which the whole of creation, and in particular man, possesses in the thought and intention of God. . . . Especially man must be given and restored to God if he is to be fully restored to himself."[31]

Easter's good news proclaims the resurrection of humanity's oneness with God and with one another in Christ. God did not raise up the spirit of God clothed in a facade of human appearance. In Christ God raised humanity to the dignity of sharing the glory of God, that is, humanity restored to its image and likeness. This is the risen humanity where "[the rulers of the earth] will fight against the Lamb, but the Lamb will conquor them" (Rev 17:14). When the rulers of this world wage war on humanity risen in Christ, they face the victorious Lamb of God.

Easter calls us to enter battle with this world's rulers not with the weapons of war but with the paschal mystery of Christ's way, truth, and life. Easter calls us to die to this world's identity of perishability so that the imperishability of God's glory might be mirrored in our own glory. This holy season celebrates the good news that through Christ, with Christ, and in Christ humanity is our salvation.

QUESTIONS FOR YOUR REFLECTION

1. What is the problem with this frequently used statement: "I'm not a saint, I'm only human"?

2. Reconciliation, forgiveness, healing, and peacemaking are works of the Church's redemptive mission. In what way is the "face of God" seen in these works?

3. Why is the Christian pursuit of oneness with God and one another a most exalted vocation?

4. How would you show that through an understanding of this meaning of vocation, the vocations of single life, marriage, religious life, and priesthood might be better understood and more fruitful?

Church Unity: Gone with the Fish?

WORD

> "Though many, we are one body, and members of one
> another, united by Christ in the bonds of love. 'Christ has
> made Jesus and Gentiles one by breaking down the barrier
> that divided us and abolishing the law with its precepts and
> decrees.' This is why we should all be of one mind and if
> one member suffers some misfortune, all should suffer with
> him; if one member is honored, all should be glad" (St. Cyril
> of Alexandria, bishop).[32]

REFLECTION

When abstinence from meat on Friday was no longer required,
someone quipped, "There goes Church unity, gone with the fish!"

For centuries, the practice of abstaining from meat on Fridays had
been regarded as a mark of Church unity. Similarly, other externals
also signified oneness of Church identity. For example, the rite of the
Tridentine Mass with its uniform use of Latin stood as a sign of Church
unity throughout the world. When that rite was changed, many of its
adherents allowed themselves to be separated from communion with
the Holy See rather than follow its directives concerning the externals
of worship.

Changes in externals have challenged us to discern the deeper
meaning of oneness which marks the Church's identity. Gradually it has
dawned on us that Church unity arises from within. Praiseworthy and
necessary as externals are, their uniform practice—imposed, enforced,
and regulated from the outside—are really not the bondedness which
is the substance of Christ's oneness with God and humanity. If the reality of God's oneness cannot be found within us, the use of externals
can hardly be called celebration.

Jesus Christ came into the world as the visible, tangible appearance
of God's hiddenness. He came to be the sacrament of who God is and
what God does, and he calls us to be instruments of that sacramental-

75

ity in the world. Our oneness as the living sacrament of God's presence is the source of the external marks that celebrate ecclesial unity. To live as models of God's identity is far more pertinent to the Church's visibility of God's oneness than the uniformity of eating fish on Friday or ritualizing the Eucharist in a language no one can understand.

In the Eucharistic Prayer of Reconciliation the Church prays, "Father make your Church throughout the world a sign of unity and an instrument of your peace."[33]

This prayer challenges us to ask, "What is the sign of this unity?" St. Cyril responds, "He [Jesus] came into this world in human flesh, not to be served, but, as he himself said, to serve God and to give his life as a ransom for many."[34]

Isaiah gives no weight to a religion of externals only:

"What care I for the number of your sacrifices?
    says the LORD.
I have had enough of whole-burnt rams
    and fat of fatlings;
In the blood of calves, lambs and goats
    I find no pleasure (Isa 1:11).

After enumerating the externals in which God finds no pleasure, Isaiah points to what does bring pleasure to God:

Put away your misdeeds from before my eyes;
    cease doing evil; learn to do good.
Make justice your aim: redress the wronged,
    hear the orphan's plea, defend the widow (Isa 1:16-17).

The Church of Christ displays the mark of authentic unity when all of her members follow the Christ who "came into this world in human flesh . . . to serve God and to give his life as a ransom for many." A life of serving God and humankind is the mark that brings pleasure to the eyes of God. Church members who "make justice [their] aim" have the sign of unity that is the criterion for salvation before God's judgment seat: "I assure you, as often as you did it for . . . my least [ones], you did it for me" (Matt 25:40).

As long as the Church unites to serve the poor and the oppressed, its unity will never be "gone with the fish."

QUESTIONS FOR YOUR REFLECTION

1. What is the difference between unity and uniformity?

2. In what way is diversity a requirement for unity?

3. When do externals cease to be effective signs of faith?

4. The Eucharist is called the "sacrament of unity." How does the gathering of people for worship challenge them to be signs of unity in their daily lives?

FIFTH SUNDAY OF EASTER

The Glory of Abandonment

WORD

> *"Babylon the great city*
> *shall be cast down . . . with violence*
> *and nevermore be found! . . .*
> *Let us rejoice and be glad,*
> *and give him glory!*
> *For this is the wedding day of the Lamb;*
> *his bride has prepared herself for the wedding"* (Rev 18:21; 19:7).

REFLECTION

When John describes his visions of heaven, he carefully couches their meanings in an imagery that invites discernment. For his contemporary readers "Babylon" relates not to the already fallen Babylon of past times but to the Roman Empire, where he foretells that in a matter of time,

> No light from a burning lamp
> shall ever again shine out in you! (Rev 18:23).

But John's designation for "Babylon" does not end with Rome. His inspired word takes us more deeply into the mystery of God's loving concern for us than his historical information about "Babylon's" fall. The Book of Revelation invites us to ask, what is the "Babylon" in us that can spoil our "wedding day [with] the Lamb"?

St. Maximus of Turin sheds light on this question: "The light of Christ is an endless day that knows no night. . . . By this we are meant to understand that the coming of Christ's light puts Satan's darkness to flight, leaving no place for any shadow of sin."[35]

The "Babylon" of our lives is the darkness of sin. The Book of Revelation pleads with us to recognize within ourselves the presence of Satan ceaselessly working to dethrone the reign of Christ. For St. John the reign of Satan was the spirit "of the world"; for St. Paul it was "the flesh." However named, the reign of Satan's "Babylon" is real and, if it be our choice, can extinguish "the light of Christ, [the] endless day that knows no night."

The Book of Revelation, however, does not contain a message of despair. Read with the eyes of faith which take us into the hidden regions of its imagery, Revelation is a book of unbounded joy. John cries out with this joy as he hears heaven's assembly sing:

> Alleluia!
> Salvation, glory and might belong to our God,
>   for his judgments are true and just!
> He has condemned the great harlot
>   who corrupted the earth with her harlotry.
> He has avenged the blood of his servants
>   which was shed by her hand. . . . Alleluia! (Rev 19:1-3).

Many readers of Revelation's joy may be genuinely perplexed. I refer to many devout men and women who have suffered tragedies in their lives. Death, rejection, illness, failure, the spectacle of scandal among their loved ones, are hardly the occasions of the joy that compel us to shout "Alleluia!" In place of joy, there reigns a deep sense of God's abandonment. The afflicted share a companionship with Christ's cry of abandonment from the cross: "My God, my God, why have you forsaken me?" (Mark 15:34).

This apparent inconsistency between Revelation's joyful Alleluias in heaven and the griefs of holy men and women who carry crosses of tragedy here upon earth is not left unaddressed by St. John:

> The angel then said to me: "Write this down: Happy are they who
> have been invited to the wedding feast of the Lamb!" The angel

continued, "These words are true; they come from God." I fell at his feet to worship him, but he said to me, "No, get up! I am merely a fellow servant with you and your brothers who give witness to Jesus. Worship God alone. The prophetic spirit proves itself by witnessing to Jesus" (Rev 19:9).

John's disclosure of this vision proclaims that we are servant exiles here on earth. We do not belong here! We live here only to prepare ourselves for "the wedding feast of the Lamb." Seen in this light, then, our experiences of abandonment are signs that God is very near. In them God calls us to the longing that prepares us for our eternal belonging with God. Our feelings of abandonment are but the voice of Jesus crying out in our humanity, "My God, my God, why have you forsaken me?" Our felt forsakenness is the very intimacy with God we imagine to be nonexistent. Indeed, the very fact that we feel abandoned is the sign that we are letting go of this world's spirit. Faith invites us to believe that!

This is one of Easter's joyful insights. Easter proclaims that Christ is raised up from our tragedies. The faith that invites us to believe this apparent paradox enables us to rejoice with heaven's assembly at the wedding feast of the Lamb. Even amidst our tears, the conviction that God reigns in our feelings of abandonment compels us to sing, "Alleluia!"

QUESTIONS FOR YOUR REFLECTION

1. When it comes to carrying our cross, why is faith a necessary deterrent to despair?

2. In what way do feelings of abandonment signal God's closeness to us? What precisely is the abandonment you are experiencing?

3. Feelings of abandonment are really signs of a deeply felt craving to belong. What is the belonging that enables us to live peacefully and joyfully in the midst of tragedy?

Nothing Less Than a Stradivarius

WORD

"The heavens were opened, and as I looked on, a white horse appeared; its rider was called 'The Faithful and True.' Justice is his standard in passing judgment and in waging war" (Rev 19:11).

REFLECTION

Handing me his violin, my father pointed to a name stamped inside its frame. It read, "Stradivarius." I looked at my father and gasped, "is this the real McCoy?" "No," he laughed, "and it isn't a real Stradivarius either."

He explained that the violin's maker probably resorted to pretense in order to compare his workmanship to that of Antonio Stradivarius. "He got away with sales tactics like this," he said, "because he knew that fiddlers like me haven't the money for 'the real McCoy.' "

It has been fifty-three years since my near encounter with the "real McCoy" of the violin world. I still possess my father's violin pretense, but I have never seen or touched a Stradivarius made in the image and likeness of its maker.

That violin never ceases to warn me against settling for pretense. The discrepancy between what its stamped name claims and what the violin really is, is a judgment against its authenticity. When such discrepancy appears in human identity, lack of integrity will be the judgment.

At the climax of John's vision of heaven, he sees a white horse mounted with a rider who is called "The Faithful and True." This name speaks of integrity. Contrasted with "Babylon" and its arrogant claims of sovereignty, the rider called "The Faithful and True" stands out in bold relief as the triumph of God's lordship. His word matches his deeds, and because of his integrity God raises up the "rider," Jesus Christ, to be humanity's sign of transformation. Christ's integrity, his oneness of word and deed, becomes God's standard for passing judgment on all humanity.

The death and resurrection of Jesus remains as the criterion for humanity's thirst to be authentic. Jesus' death on the cross signaled an end to the pretense of this world's claims that its values, ideals, and goods are humanity's true worth. This pretense found its judgment in Christ's death on the cross: Nothing of this world came to Christ's rescue. Christ was rescued after he died by this world's Creator, whose resurrection deed revealed a consistency with Christ's resurrection word: "Destroy this temple . . . and in three days I will raise it up" (John 2:19). That's the integrity that destroyed the power of hell!

Jesus' resurrection became humanity's authentic identity. The Church cries out, "This is the day the LORD has made" (Ps 118:24), not a day of twenty-four hours but the "day" of a never-ending testament that Christ's risen humanity is also our humanity. Indeed, Christ's resurrection is humanity's "Faithful and True" identity, which fully began one day two thousand years ago. That day was real. Likewise real is the certainty that all who commit themselves to the pilgrimage of Christ's paschal mystery will be transformed into the likeness of Christ's resurrection.

By what standard will we be judged? We shall be judged by the evidence of integrity in our lives. When there appears no discrepancy between what we say we believe and how we live what we say, this marriage of word and deed will be the standard by which God will judge us. That judgment will be fruit of the evidence that we have traveled the pilgrimage of Christ's death and resurrection. Integrity will be the witness that we have died to this world's pretense and raised by God to the truth of Christ's resurrection.

To come, then, into God's presence clothed in the garments of Christ's resurrection is to come as the "day the LORD has made." Our surrender to God's loving power of resurrection finds us completely enveloped in the new reality of our transformation. St. Gregory of Nyssa exclaims: "On this day is created the true man, the man made in the image and likeness of God. For 'this day the LORD has made' is the beginning of a new world. Of this day the prophet says that it is not like other days."[36]

It is because of "this day" that my father's violin continuously reminds me, "Don't settle for pretense!"

QUESTIONS FOR YOUR REFLECTION

1. Be honest with yourself! What pretenses indict your practice of Christianity with a less than "real McCoy" authenticity? Examples?

2. Be honest again! What are the evidences that your practice of Christianity will be the judgment that you are "The Faithful and True?" Examples?

3. Christianity that concentrates only on externals with no evidence of a lived paschal mystery is pretense. How is this assertion related to Christ's words, "None of those who cry out, 'Lord, Lord,' will enter the kingdom of heaven, but only the one who does the will of my Father in heaven" (Matt 7:21)?

4. From your observations of others whose witness of Christ's life has been deeply moving, what are the evidences of integrity in their lives? Give some specific examples.

TUESDAY OF THE FIFTH WEEK

Branches, Not Vines, Bear Fruit

WORD

> *"From Christ and in Christ, we have been reborn through the Spirit in order to bear the fruit of a new life founded upon our faith in him and our love for him"* (St. Cyril of Alexandria, bishop).[37]

REFLECTION

Lest our spirituality become static, it is imperative that we understand the meaning of mystery. Mystery is about hiddenness, not unexplainability. The mystery of God is the hiddenness of God longing to be revealed so that humankind might "taste and see how good the LORD is . . . " (Ps 34:9).

Jesus' parable about the vine and the branches touches on God as mystery and on our role as sharers in its revelation:

"I am the vine, you are the branches.
He who lives in me and I in him,
will produce abundantly,
for apart from me you can do nothing" (John 15:5).

In this parable Jesus leaves no doubt that humankind's role is to bear witness to God's hidden identity. Clusters of grapes do not sprout forth from the trunks of vines; they hang from their branches. And so it is with Christ and ourselves. Jesus was sent by the Father as the hidden fullness of God's presence. Like the vine, he embodies God's hidden fruitfulness waiting to be revealed, tasted, and nourished by all who hunger for God's goodness. Jesus came to call us to be his branches and to bear the fruitfulness of God's hidden presence. Incredible as that seems, it is true. God created us to be witnesses of the abundance that Christ was sent to reveal. "From Christ and in Christ, we have been reborn through the Spirit in order to bear the fruit of a new life."

The hiddenness of God's love becomes visible not by way of apparitions but by way of its embodiment in our humanity. Christ's Church is the sacrament of this embodiment. Christ is the Church's vine and we are her branches. In the Church, vine and branches are united by God's Spirit in the strongest possible intimacy. It is from this intimacy that the infinite fruitfulness of God's treasury of strength, healing, mercy, and forgiveness flows into the branches for the availability of all.

A remembrance of a childhood incident which bore the fruit of repentance never fails to move me. That repentance came by way of my mother's glance on a terribly hot day. The five of us children preferred to remain indoors away from the blazing sun's heat, but the heat of the house was hardly an antidote for the restlessness and irritability that made life unpleasant for our tired mother. In the midst of the fray my mother glanced at me. I was forever changed by the sorrow that swept over me as I beheld her hurt face.

Speechless, I ran off to my room and, from behind the closed door, poured out tears of repentance. In my mother's glance I had discovered more than a look of hurt; I had discovered the witness of a mother's love and fidelity that prevailed despite her children's ingratitude. For the first time in my life I had touched a reality which, though fully present in my mother, was hidden by my own unawareness and unconcern for the beauty of her love. That unawareness was transformed into a deep concern when I discovered in my mother's glance that we were really loved! That moment bore, for this small child, the fruit of a changed life into whose center was welcomed the fruit of genuine love and fidelity.

My mother's glance was the reality in which I saw God, and it changed my life. Her glance became the branch that bore the fruit of repentance. Through her, the very hiddenness of God's gentleness and tenderness offered me the gift of conversion. I accepted.

Jesus came that we might be sacraments of God's hiddenness seeking to be unveiled in the branches of our humanity. Jesus said:

"I solemnly assure you,
the man who has faith in me
will do the works I do,
and greater far than these.
Why? Because I go to the Father" (John 14:12).

We will do the works that Christ did "and greater far than these" because he sent his Spirit, freed of the limitations of time and space, to do in us what "was lacking . . . in Christ" (Col 1:24). God's Spirit is the presence of God, who binds the branches to the vine so that God's hiddenness might be continuously unveiled for the world to embrace. We are the branches whose daily fidelity to our baptismal commitment enables us to be the fruitfulness and the sacramentality which Christ's limitations of time and space were unable to reveal. Our humanity, graced with the presence of God's Spirit, continues the fruitfulness of Christ's ongoing mission in the world. Indeed, branches, not vines, bear fruit!

QUESTIONS FOR YOUR REFLECTION

1. An understanding of mystery as hiddenness preserves our spirituality from becoming static. Why does mystery as unexplainability make straight the way to a static spirituality?

2. Why does our resignation to mystery as unexplainability endanger our fruit-bearing role in Christ's parable of the vine and the branches?

3. Jesus said that with faith we "will do the works I do, and greater far than these." What are examples of far-greater works done by Christians over the past two thousand years?

4. In your own life, who are those who have borne the fruits of conversion for you?

Why Are They Like This?

WORD

"Christians are indistinguishable from other men [and women] either by nationality, language or customs. . . . And yet, there is something extraordinary about their lives" (A Letter to Diognetus).[38]

"[God] shall dwell with them and they shall be his people and he shall be their God who is always with them" (Rev 21:3).

REFLECTION

A young man wanted his love for Jesus to distinguish him from others. He chose to dress like Jesus and to grow a beard along the lines of some of the artistic portrayals he had seen. For a while he succeeded in looking like the Jesus he imagined. In time, however, his appearance was gradually taken for granted. Those who saw him every day exiled him to the land of the "quaint" and the "irrelevant." The distinctiveness of his "love for Jesus" went no deeper than the shallowness that others ascribed to his difference.

In terms of what is seen in Christians' appearance, they are "indistinguishable from other men [and women] either by nationality, language or customs." The difference that Christians make lies not in their external appearances but in their devotedness to Christ, whom they have placed at the center of their lives. This centrality makes it quite apparent that "something extraordinary" radiates from them. In his apostolic exhortation "On Evangelization in the Modern World" Pope Paul VI writes: "[They] radiate in an altogether simple and unaffected way their faith in values that go beyond current values, and their hope in something that is not seen and that one would not dare imagine."[39]

Here, Pope Paul VI confirms that the distinctiveness of Christians arises from a realm beyond what can be humanly conceived, perceived, and received. The source of their distinctiveness cannot be seen, touched, or imagined. Rather they live by the power of faith and hope which convinces all who see them that the substance of their distinctiveness is real.

Unlike the young man who dressed according to his imagination of Christ, true Christians are never taken for granted. Nor did Pope Paul VI take for granted the distinguishing factors of witness by which they are noticed: "These Christians stir up irresistible questions in the hearts of those who see how they live: Why are they like this? Why do they live this way? Who or what is it that inspires them? Why are they in our midst?"[40]

True Christians do not seek to be different in appearance or even to arouse "irresistible questions" from others. It is their conviction that what is seen as different in the eyes of people is normative in the eyes of God. With the eyes of faith and hope "fixed on Jesus" (Heb 12:2), "they live in their own countries as though they were only passing through."[41] Faith and hope offer Christians the substance of God's vision for humanity. John writes: "I . . . saw a new Jerusalem, the holy city, coming down out of heaven from God. . . . I heard a loud voice from the throne cry out: 'This is God's dwelling among men. He shall dwell with them and they shall be his people and he shall be their God who is always with them'" (Rev. 21:2-3).

The "new Jerusalem" is a people who have chosen to live according to values that "go beyond current values." Among these people can be found, for example, those who choose celibacy, poverty, and obedience as their way of living. They choose to give witness to values that many consider irrelevant. They seek by the practice of these vows to make believable that chastity, simplicity, and obedience are possible for *all* who choose to share companionship with Christ in the "new Jerusalem."

If those who choose to live a vowed life "stir up irresistible questions," then these questions are an invitation to pursue the reasons for a vowed life. Those who dismiss celibacy, poverty, and obedience as irrelevant reveal the extent to which they have succumbed to values that perish. If vows appear to be irrelevant to some, it may be that this world's values at the center of their existence have smugly *proclaimed* them irrelevant. If a vowed life appears to be different, well, it is! The difference that vows make is their rootedness in a life far beyond this world's perishability. The world demands only the dubious distinction of conformity.

God's hidden presence begs that we remove from the center of our lives anything that allows only the difference of perishability. God longs to be our center so that we may be transformed into the imperishability of God's image. Our total surrender to God's indwelling presence does not give us a new nationality, a new language, or new customs. Transformation takes place in our personhood where "something extraordinary about [our] lives" arouses "irresistible questions." As temples of God's indwelling presence, the "new Jerusalem" will make the difference that no one will ever take for granted.

QUESTIONS FOR YOUR REFLECTION

1. The door to God's hiddenness is kept open by a distinctiveness that provides a Catholic identity. What are some interior marks of identity that ought to characterize the body of Christ?

2. What values prized by Catholicism draw both criticism and persecution from those who feel threatened by Catholic distinctiveness?

3. What person in your life aroused in you irresistible questions about why he or she was different?

4. Why have poverty, celibacy, and obedience been regarded by some as irrelevant?

THURSDAY OF THE FIFTH WEEK

But It Doesn't Make Sense!

WORD

"*I saw no temple in the city. The Lord, God the Almighty, is its temple—he and the Lamb*" (Rev 21:22).

"*When Christ told the crowds that they must eat his flesh and drink his blood, they were horrified and began to murmur among themselves: 'This teaching is too hard; who can be expected to listen to it?'*" (St. Gaudentius of Brescia, bishop).[42]

REFLECTION

The cancer that threatens faith is relevance. Within its narrow boundaries lies the attitude that if something doesn't make sense, then why believe it? To wit:

"It doesn't make sense for a woman to give birth to an unborn life she doesn't want. Abortion makes more sense, doesn't it?"

"It doesn't make sense for the terminally ill to go on living if they are no longer useful to the world. Euthanasia makes more sense, doesn't it?"

"It doesn't make sense to require celibacy for those who devote most of their lives to the married and their families. Marriage for priests and religious makes more sense, doesn't it?"

"It doesn't make sense for a couple to have more than one or two children in a society where having a large family is unaffordable. Birth control makes more sense, doesn't it?"

"It doesn't make sense to let murderers live when they have deprived their victims of life. Capital punishment makes more sense, doesn't it?"

These examples of relevance give evidence of a reasoning that measures God's way of viewing truth according to the reasoning that tailors faith to *our* way of viewing truth. The truth of the matter is, faith which "makes sense" is really not faith at all. Faith begins when understanding seeks faith's light at the point where this world's "light" of relevance becomes darkness.

Faith and relevance are incompatible because faith and mystery are intimately one. Far more of God's presence lies hidden within us than what relevance has the capacity to understand and embrace. Faith is a gift of God enabling us to accept without understanding the transcendence of God, for

"Eye has not seen, ear has not heard,
  nor has it so much as dawned on man
  what God has prepared for those who love him" (1 Cor 2:9).

Faith's joy is the deep conviction that what we can't understand or find relevant is, nevertheless, the reality that "God has prepared for those who love him."

The hiddenness of God's presence in Jesus proved to be the stumbling block for those who found his message irrelevant. They turned away from Jesus at the point where Jesus did not make sense to them.

The Eucharist, for example, proved to be a decisive point where they turned away. The decision to walk no longer with Jesus was based on their inability to make sense of his assertion, "I am the bread of life" (John 6:48). Jesus insisted,

"I myself am the living bread
come down from heaven.
If anyone eats this bread
he shall live forever;
the bread I will give
is my flesh, for the life of the world" (John 6:51).

These words touched only the ears of many listeners. They were unable to hear—beyond their understanding of the relevance that deprived them of a happiness that "eye has not seen [nor] ear . . . heard." St. Gaudentius observes, "When Christ told the crowds that they must eat his flesh and drink his blood, they were horrified and began to murmur among themselves: 'This teaching is too hard; who can be expected to listen to it?'"

Jesus refused to compromise or to soften a teaching too hard for them to endure (see John 6:60). He did not cave in to the demands of would-be disciples for a relevancy that met their standards of understanding. Jesus spoke in the realm of faith. His vision of "relevance" went far beyond the Law's specifications for belief. He stood his ground and replied to the accusations of his "hard" sayings. He asked, "Does it shake your faith?" (John 6:61).

The celebration of the Eucharist invites us to look beyond the appearances of bread and wine so that our faith may carry us into a fuller presence of Christ. Faith in Christ's sacramental presence calls us to believe in Christ's hidden but real presence in the countless ways this world's standards declares to be irrelevant. The Eucharist beckons us to pay attention to that which "doesn't make sense" according to *our* measurements of judgment so that *God's* measurements of judgment may become real and felt in our lives.

QUESTIONS FOR YOUR REFLECTION

1. How is the "pick and choose" version of practicing one's religion a sign of the "cancer" of relevancy?

2. Why are faith and "making sense" incompatible?

3. The people of the United States take pride in being pragmatic. When does pragmatism as a nation's basic philosophy become a threat to faith?

Sooner Than I Thought

WORD

"Remember, I am coming soon! Happy the man who heeds the prophetic message of this book!" (Rev 22:7).

REFLECTION

My mother prepared a dinner for the celebration of my ordination anniversary. Little did I know that it was to be a "sting."

Shortly before leaving for my mother's home, two dear friends, Moira and Leo, called their congratulations from New York. After we chatted for awhile, I urged them to visit us in Iowa. Moira responded, "We are planning to come soon."

The prospect delighted me. As we brought our conversation to an end, Moira again said, "Don't forget, we are coming soon."

When I arrived at my mother's home, cheers of "Happy anniversary!" greeted me. I responded to their good wishes, "I too have some cheery news; Moira and Leo just called from New York to let me know that they are coming to see us soon." Suddenly, Leo and Moira walked into the room, and Moira blurted out, "I told you we would be coming soon!" I had been stung! They were already here.

The focal point of John's Revelation is the good news that God's coming is not a future event. God is already in our midst. That's not a sting. But why did God say to John, "Remember, I am coming soon"? If God is already in our midst, why the "soon" that is yet to come? The answer lies not in God's coming but in our coming to the awareness of God's presence in our midst.

We relate to God by faith because God's fullness is infinitely more than we can humanly experience. Patiently and gradually, faith leads us to realms of divine presence we can only realize gradually. As faith waits for our yet-to-be awakening, this waiting forces God to say, "I am coming soon!"

While faith enables us to accept the good news that God is already in our midst, it does not demand that we fully experience the joy of God's presence now. Faith must never be discarded simply because we don't "feel" joy or sing "Alleluia" with the fervor of heaven's awareness of God. Faith is the quiet conviction that one's "I am" is rooted in God's "I Am."

Reaching its climactic conclusion, the Book of Revelation confirms faith's focal premise that human existence has meaning only in God. "[God's servants] shall see him face to face and bear his name on their foreheads. . . . Worship God alone!" (Rev 22:4, 9). Not even faith and hope will be needed in heaven because God's servants will fully embrace heaven's eternal glory. "They will need no light from lamps or the sun, for the Lord God shall give them light, and they shall reign forever" (Rev 22:5).

The perspective that God's coming is "future" is evidence of our spiritual dullness. Faith leads us to the quiet unfolding of God's presence as we joyfully discover that God's "soon" is really God's "I Am." For now, our "I am" must wait amidst the earthly realities that see God's coming only as a future reality.

Faith is a buffer zone between the full realization of Christ's vision of happiness and our yet-to-be realization of its vision. On the night before he died, Jesus prayed that all may be one,

> "as you, Father, are in me, and I in you;
> I pray that they may be [one] in us
> . . . as we are one" (John 17:21-22).

Faith enables us to pass over from a oneness of "togetherness" to a oneness of identity. It is of the latter that Blessed Isaac writes:

> Just as the head and body of a man form one single man, so the Son of the virgin and those he has chosen to be his members form a single man and the one Son of Man. . . . Therefore the whole body with its head is the Son of Man, Son of God, and [one with] God. This is the explanation of the Lord's words: "Father, I desire that as you and I are one, so they may be one with us."[43]

QUESTIONS FOR YOUR REFLECTION

1. In what way does marriage signify the oneness of the wedding and the oneness of the marriage? What is the difference between "wedding" and "marriage"?

2. Faith leads us to the certainty of hope. From our reflection on the Book of Revelation, what is the one certainty that God's gift of hope guarantees?

3. We hear it said, "I no longer feel religious; I think I'm losing my faith." How would you respond to that remark?

4. Easter's paschal mystery of rising and dying is pertinent to the observation that faith is a "buffer zone." In this zone where faith asks us to accept what we can't fully realize, what is the dying we are asked to endure? What is the rising we can expect?

SATURDAY OF THE FIFTH WEEK

Coming Soon? Amen!

WORD

"Amen! Come Lord Jesus!" (Rev 22:20).

"Our thoughts in this present life should turn on the praise of God" (St. Augustine, bishop).[44]

REFLECTION

God's final promise to John in the Book of Revelation begs one word of response: "Amen!"

"Amen" is much more than a spoken or written word. It is an unconditional commitment to pass over from the loves of this world's gods to the love of God alone. This passover, this deliverance of ourselves into the lordship of Jesus Christ, is the praise of God which St. Augustine suggests as the center around which "our thoughts in this present life should turn." Our vocation is our "Amen," through which praise of God liberates us from any indebtedness to this world's vocation to perishability.

God asks no "things" from us as the substance of sacrifice:

> What care I for for the number of your sacrifices?
> says the LORD (Isa 1:11).

God asks only for the "Amen" of our total selves, which leads to the transformation of our identities. That transformation of those committed to be Christ's ecclesial presence clearly and unmistakably reveals the characteristics of Christ's identity. Christ is prophet, priest, and king. We fittingly praise God when the face of Christ can be clearly seen on the face of the Church. What does it mean, then, for us to share in the prophetic, priestly, and kingly identity of Jesus Christ?

A prophet is one whose life "speaks God." When the witness of our lives speaks God, the Church witnesses Christ's identity and his prophetic witness of God. For all eternity, God has spoken only one Word—Jesus. That Word is Christ's "Amen" to God's power and presence. When the lives of her united members, free of indebtedness to this world's perishability, radiate God's power and presence, we speak God with the prophetic "Amen" of our sacrificial lives.

To be priestly is to mediate God. Mediation means that humanity, graced to be the identity of Jesus' power and presence, becomes the instrument through which God can be revealed to the whole world. "Amen" is our graced consent to be the mediation of God's Word, our acceptance of the baptismal responsibility of sharing in Christ's priesthood. We acknowledge that responsibility when we gather around the Church's priests, who lead God's people in celebrating baptism's priestly commitment. This is the praise that God finds pleasing.

The kingship of Christ is his response to the mission of servanthood. His lordship is not one of being served but of serving others (see Mark 10:45). The kingship of Christ springs from his deeply felt kinship with the lowly. His call for discipleship asks of us a permanent commitment to be sharers in his servanthood. He calls his followers to share their lives with all who hunger and thirst for human dignity. This dedication to the poor, this sharing in Christ's servanthood, is the third way that our lives become the sacrifice of praise pleasing to God.

The evidence of these three characteristics of Christ indelibly stamped on the Church's identity is our "Amen!" It is the Church's praise, making evident our awareness that God is already in our midst. The Church's prophetic, priestly, and kingly roles are the marks of the Lamb's identity, clearly setting the Church apart as God's new Jerusalem, his foundation of peace.

Here, then, is the praise God invites us to bring to worship. God begs us to celebrate the "witness to all who hear the prophetic words of [Revelation]" (Rev 22:18). God begs that we, the body of Christ, become sacraments of Christ's light—the light of his Word, his priestliness, and his servanthood. "Through him, with him, in him, in the unity of the Holy Spirit, all glory and honor are yours, Almighty Father, for ever and ever. Amen."[45]

QUESTIONS FOR YOUR REFLECTION

1. Our response to "Body of Christ" as we receive the sacrament of Christ's body in Communion is "Amen." What is the commitment the Eucharist's "Amen" asks of us?

2. In the sacramental context of eating and drinking, what do these sacramental appearances signify in terms of our hearing God's Word? How is this significance related to "Amen"?

3. Can you list some concrete examples of "speaking God," mediating God, and serving God that enable the Church to witness Christ's identity in the world?

4. Easter's joy of Passover's rising also proclaims the pain of Passover's dying in our lives. To speak God, what must we die speaking of? To mediate God, to what must we die revealing? To serve God and others, to what must we die serving?

5. What is the resurrection that our prophetic, priestly, and kingly lives can anticipate?

The Missing Link

WORD

". . . we speak of the word of life.
(This life became visible;
we have seen and bear witness to it;
and we proclaim to you the eternal life
that was present to the Father
and became visible to us)" (1 John 1:1-2).

REFLECTION

No teaching about the Church's identity puzzled me more than the four marks of the Church: one, holy, catholic, and apostolic. The source of my puzzlement may have been the absence of a linkage, by which I failed to see the intimacy between the Church and her founder, Jesus Christ. I gave mental assent to the definitional role of the four marks but found missing their linkage to the personhood of Jesus Christ, her founder. This missing link impeded my understanding of their role in linking the Church to Christ.

Reflecting on my perplexity concerning the four marks of the Church, a perplexity that plagued me well into my priesthood, I recognize now that it sprang from a narrow perspective of viewing the Church solely from its institutional model. This perspective gave the four marks of the Church an organizational image rather than one of a living organism. Within this institutional frame of reference, I regarded the four marks of the Church as criteria for defining the Church's institutional identity.

Throughout my education, I searched for the missing link, the hinge by which the marks of the Church might become more than institutional determinants of our relationship with Jesus Christ. For me, the missing link turned out to be the Church's capacity to embody the identity of Jesus as prophet, priest, and servant. I reasoned that the four marks of the Church were not criteria by which we authenticate the Church's institutional identity. Rather, they are marks of *fruitfulness,*

95

whereby God's Spirit *verifies* the Church as Christ's prophetic, priestly, and servant identity.

The four marks of the Church, then, are not conditions that indicate institutional authenticity. They are the fruits that bear witness to the truth of a people who have committed themselves to the vocation of becoming Christ's prophetic, priestly, and servant identity. Christ's last will and testament (see John 17:21) was of a oneness with his threefold identity, whereby the Church might be marked with unity, holiness, catholicity, and apostolicity.

The "true Church" comprises those who pursue the vocation of being the threefold identity of Christ. Their membership does not repudiate the institutional model of Church identity because they do not forget that the ecclesial presence of Christ is both human and divine. Those who reject the Church's institutional modality under the illusion that it stands in the way of her divine identity sow the seeds of the "do your own thing" anarchy.

As bearers, then, of Christ's threefold identity, our baptismal commitment to Christ carries the responsibility of mirroring the fruits of that identity. These are not marks that *we* initiate; they are the evidences of God's indwelling presence in those whose faith calls them to respond. They flow from God's Spirit transforming the Church into the identity of Christ the prophet, Christ the priest, and Christ the servant.

Someone wrote that religion means "relinking." The joy of Easter is the good news that Christ's resurrection has enabled a relinking, marking the Church with unity, holiness, catholicity, and apostolicity. These marks give evidence that

> we have fellowship with one another,
> and the blood of his Son Jesus (1 John 1:7).

QUESTIONS FOR YOUR REFLECTION

1. How does the institutional model of the Church as one's sole perspective of ecclesial identity pose a threat to her teaching regarding the four marks of the Church?

2. Why, then, must institution be a necessary model of Church identity?

3. In order for the Church's four marks to be visible and effective, why is it necessary for us to begin with Christ as prophet, Christ as priest, and Christ as servant, as the Church's linkage with Christ?

4. Without any reference to Christ's triune identity, how would a sole preoccupation with the Church's four marks not be in her best interests in terms of her relationship with Christ?

5. In the light of our reflection on the four marks of the Church, what are your observations on this text from the Second Vatican Council: "The human race has passed from a rather static concept of reality to a more dynamic, evolutionary one."[46]

6. In what way would a "static concept of reality" contribute to a perplexity about the four marks of the Church, in terms of ecclesial identity?

MONDAY OF THE SIXTH WEEK

The Return to Our Original Beauty

WORD

"Finding us in a state of deformity, The Spirit restores our original beauty and fills us with his grace, leaving no room for anything unworthy of our love" (Didymus of Alexandria).[47]

REFLECTION

God-likeness was humankind's "original beauty." God created all men and women for no other purpose than to be the center of their existence. When the fruit of this world became their preoccupation, however, the beast of human deformity became their center. Because of that deformity, God sent the Spirit to restore "our original beauty [filling] us with his grace, leaving no room for anything unworthy of our love."

Lapses into deformity happen when we prize rationales for human existence rather than the truth of God's centrality in our lives. As this world's spirit inches closer and closer to the center of our lives, we gradually become comfortable with its "state of deformity."

The opening chapters of Genesis are an account of a passover in reverse. The first three chapters record that humankind passed from a state of original beauty to a state of original deformity. Created in the image and likeness of God (see Gen 1:26), Adam and Eve were lured by the lie that God-likeness can be bestowed on humankind by the fruits of this world. "You certainly will not die! No, God knows well that the moment you eat of it your eyes will be opened and you will be like gods who know what is good and what is bad" (Gen 3:4-5).

This claim carried the arrogant inference that the fruit of the tree in "the middle of the garden" (Gen 3:3) possessed the power to endow humankind with the eternity only God possesses. Clearly, this claim, together with our inclination to fall for it, is the deformity that identifies original sin. The inconsistency of creatures falling for this lie threatens the existence which God destined: to be in the likeness of God. Adam and Eve's conduct lacked the integrity that marked a wholesome relationship between Creator and creature.

In his first Letter, St. John the Evangelist offers us the definitive standard by which we can determine the presence of integrity in our lives:

> The way we can be sure we are in union with him
> is for the man who claims to abide in him
> to conduct himself just as he did (1 John 2:5-6).

John's point is this: When there is a oneness between what we claim we believe about our oneness with Christ and the conduct that matches that claim, there radiates from us the integrity which is our "original beauty."

St. John's first Letter does not mince words about inconsistencies between oral professions and behavioral transgressions. Hence:

> The man who claims, "I have known him,"
> without keeping his commandments,
> is a liar; in such a one there is no truth.
> But whoever keeps his word,
> truly has the love of God been made perfect in him (1 John 2:4-5).

Easter's message calls us to the restoration of integrity's original beauty. We are called to a conversion whereby we die to the lie that creaturehood is *equal* to creatorship so that we might be raised to the "original beauty" of God's claim that creaturehood was created *in the image and likeness* of God. That conversion pilgrimage is the Passover mystery which Easter celebrates.

God as the centerpiece of our lives is the new commandment that sums up all other commandments. When Christ has become the center of our lives, we experience the light of God's love. That light will radiate when the evidence of consistency between words of faith and deeds of love marks our integrity:

> The man who continues in the light
> is the one who loves his brother;
> there is nothing in him to cause a fall (1 John 2:10).

The "love of God has been poured out in our hearts through the Holy Spirit . . ." (Rom 5:5). The Easter season contains the joyful proclamation that God's indwelling Spirit groans to lead us from the deformity of life whose image is ashes to the beauty of life whose image is God.

QUESTIONS FOR YOUR REFLECTION

1. From the words of Didymus regarding "a state of deformity," what deeper meaning can be derived from the word "reform"? When written as "re-form," how does it relate to Christ as the center of our lives?

2. Read St. Matthew's account of the rich man asking Jesus, "What good must I do to possess everlasting life?" (Matt 19:16-22). What inconsistency did the man display between his perspective of perfection and that of Jesus?

3. In what way is creaturehood the key to our possession of God's "original beauty"?

4. A conversion is a radical change in one's life. How would you connect conversion with Easter's perspective of Passover?

Eucharist: Sacrament of Unity

WORD

"If, in Christ, all of us, both ourselves and he who is within us by his own flesh, are members of the same body, is it not clear that we are one, both with one another and with Christ? He is the bond that unites us, because he is at once both God and man" (St. Cyril of Alexandria, bishop).[48]

REFLECTION

The Eucharist is the sacrament of communion between "both ourselves and him who is within us." If this is our life's vocation, the Eucharist will achieve the communion that it signifies. Indeed, all of the sacraments become effective when the reality to which they call us becomes our vocation. But when our sacramental concern involves only the commitment to perform sacramental ritual, the absence of daily dedication to sacramental significance begets only ineffectiveness.

When we celebrate the sacraments, we cannot exclude their call to the issues and concerns that require care and attention. Sacraments call us to look beyond the rituals we perform so that their significance might become the *way* we address ourselves to the concerns and issues of our daily lives. To celebrate sacraments without linking them to their lived significance is to risk magic.

Built into human purpose and commitment is the capacity for relationships. Their growth and development is what it means to be alive. No sacramental endeavor can be fruitful unless we pursue the reality of the social significance of each person's "I am." When we pursue the vocation of discovering each sacrament's connection to human life's quest for communion and belonging, the meaning of our "I am" comes alive. So do the sacraments!

We are truly alive when we belong to God and one another. Religion's fundamental purpose is to awaken us to the belonging that lies beyond our earthly "I am." The sacraments celebrate the certainty that our longing for God and each other is the unmistakable sign that we belong to Christ's risen presence which the Eucharist signifies. God is the "I Am" to which we were created to belong. God is the reality that lies beyond the perishability unworthy of our ultimate belonging. St. John writes:

> Have no love for the world . . .
> the world with its seductions is passing away
> but the man who does God's will
> endures forever (1 John 2:15, 17).

The Eucharist is the handmaid of religion. In visible, concrete ways it enables the whole Church to pursue the vocation of belonging to God and to one another. How succinctly St. Cyril summarizes the Eucharist's role as handmaid to religion's call to unity: "All who receive the sacred flesh of Christ are united with him as members of his body."[49]

Again and again the Eucharist celebrates oneness. "This is the teaching of St. Paul," St. Cyril continues,

> when he speaks of the mystery of our religion "that was hidden from former generations, but has now been revealed to the holy apostles and prophets by the Spirit; namely, that the Gentiles are joint-heirs with the Jews, that they are members of the same body, and that they have a share in the promise made by God in Christ Jesus."[50]

To ignore the Eucharist is to be out of touch with the core meaning of human life. For example, those who complain that they are not getting anything out of the Mass are probably admitting that they are already suffering the isolation from God that total preoccupation with this world's perishability invariably effects. To find the Mass "strange" can only mean that one has discovered God to be a stranger:

> If anyone loves the world,
> the Father's love has no place in him (1 John 2:15).

The Eucharist invites us not to "get something out of the Mass" but to celebrate the Eucharist with the joy of being in communion with God and one another. "Eucharist" means "good gift," and the human dignity that it ennobles obliges us to gather each Sunday to give thanks to God for the good-gift communion with God that makes real the meaning of our lives. This reality of communion is what its sacrament signifies in an ecclesial setting. We come to the Eucharist as sacraments of communion in the world. This is the sacramentality that the Mass begets for us as Christ offers our wor(th)ship to the Father.

QUESTIONS FOR YOUR REFLECTION

1. When the reality that sacraments signify is absent from their celebration, what danger awaits them?

2. "Vocation" is a word often applied only to those who are ordained and consecrated for works of ministry. What is the larger meaning of vocation inherent in the sacrament of baptism?

3. How is the vocation of all the baptized signified in the other sacraments? What, for example, is the vocation of Eucharist? reconciliation? matrimony? holy orders?

4. Religion is the bonding of ourselves with God and with one another. In regard to this, how is Eucharist the "handmaid" of religion?

WEDNESDAY OF THE SIXTH WEEK

Called to Be the Fifth Gospel

WORD

"The . . . lukewarm hearts [of the disciples] were fired by the light of faith and began to burn within them as the Lord opened up the Scriptures. And as they shared their meal with him, their eyes were opened in the breaking of the bread, opened far more happily to the sight of their own glorified humanity than were the eyes of our first parents to the shame of their sin" (St. Leo the Great, pope).[51]

REFLECTION

A stonecutter, who was a nonpracticing Catholic, was asked by the parish priest to place the marble tabernacle in a new setting. Somewhat surprised to be asked, the stonecutter gladly accepted the pastor's request for his skill. It took less than an evening's work to complete the task.

The next Sunday, the stonecutter was present at Mass. Afterward he awkwardly but honestly thanked the pastor for inviting him to use his skill for the house of God. "I am back at church," he said, "because now I feel that something of myself belongs to the Church."

It was one thing for the stonecutter to acknowledge the parish's need for his skill; it was quite another that he became the fulfillment of that need. Similarly, the basics of Christian identity require not only knowledge about God's Word but also the living witness of God's Word in our personhood. Knowing *about* Christ does not bring about the embodiment of Christ's personhood, whose witness in a people transforms them.

It is one matter for us to know about the four Gospels; it is quite another that we become their fulfillment in our daily lives. The four Gospels are incomplete. They cry out for a people to be the fifth gospel. These evangelized people become the gospel's lived reality in the world.

On the way to Emmaus after his resurrection, Jesus met two of his disciples who did not recognize him. St. Luke records that the two disciples, reflecting on their experience of Christ's risen presence, exclaimed, "Were not our hearts burning inside us?" (Luke 24:32). They also acknowledged that the burning in their hearts did not bring about their recognition of Jesus. Only when Jesus broke bread and shared it with them did they experience the belonging by which they recognized his identity.

St. John the Evangelist pleads:

> Remain in him now, little ones,
> so that, when he reveals himself,
> we may be fully confident
> and not retreat in shame at his coming.
> If you consider the holiness that is his,
> you can be sure that everyone who acts in holiness
> has been begotten by him (1 John 2:28-29).

Our sense of belonging to Christ and to his Church makes imperative that we not only "consider holiness" but that we also "act in holiness." Jesus himself insisted, "None of those who cry out, 'Lord, Lord,' will enter the kingdom of God but only the one who does the will of my Father in heaven" (Matt 7:21).

St. John's warning about the coming of the Antichrist was really an admonition to those whose lives failed to be rooted in the belonging which witnesses both knowledge about Jesus and the lived experience of his life:

> It was from our ranks that they took their leave—
> not that they really belonged to us;
> for if they had belonged to us,
> they would have stayed with us.
> [Their leaving] only served to show that none of them was ours
> (1 John 2:19).

The staying power that justifies our identity with Christ's body, the Church, is the belonging we experience when we "break the bread" of our gifted personhood for Christ and his Church. It was the parish priest's recognition of a man's giftedness that enabled the stonecutter to "break the bread" of his skill, whereby he recognized the belonging for which he had hungered. The sharing of his giftedness enabled him to be reconciled to the giftedness of Christ's Eucharistic presence.

Our staying power with the Church is not assured simply by hearing the Gospels or giving them a mental nod. It is assured when we give witness to our ecclesial "Amen" in our lives. When the Church's sacramental Communion signifies our practice of Christ's four Gospels, we become Christ's fifth gospel. This is the meaning of evangelization, which ignites the fires of God's Word. When the hearts of Christians become the "light of the world" men and women will recognize Christ in "the breaking of the bread."

QUESTIONS FOR YOUR REFLECTION

1. What is the difference between our witness of Christ and the witness that is the function of our eyes?

2. How would you explain this: The Eucharist is both "noun" and "verb"?

3. As his reason that we might be one, Christ prayed "that the world may believe that you sent me" (John 17:21). How would you relate this reason with our role as "fifth gospel"?

4. How does the "breaking of the bread" refute the attitude that says, "I don't have to belong to the Church in order to belong to Christ?"

Praise God for This New Captivity

WORD

"Each of us has received God's favor in the measure in which Christ bestows it. Thus you find Scripture saying:

'When he ascended on high, he took a host of captives and gave gifts to men.'

'He ascended'—what does this mean but that he had first descended into the lower regions of the earth? He who descended is the very one who ascended high above the heavens, that he might fill all men with his gifts" (Eph 4:7-9).

REFLECTION

As American soldiers entered a Nazi concentration camp to free its captives in 1945, the fright of one victim turned to joy as he cried out, "Praise God for this new captivity!"

The joy of Christ's ascension springs from the lips of the "new captivity" which Jesus carried to the throne of God. This is the captivity of all who have surrendered themselves to the fulfillment of God's reason for creating human life. Christ's ascension into heaven is nothing less than this: All of humanity who have chosen Christ as their way of life are present in Christ before the throne of God. "Praise God for this new captivity!"

The realization of this stunning truth burned like a roaring fire in the heart of St. Paul. Again and again he endeavors to help us understand that all are called to live in a manner consistent with the dignity of being "in Christ." To the Ephesians he writes: "I plead with you, then, as a prisoner for the Lord, to live a life worthy of the calling you have received, . . . Make every effort to preserve the unity which has the Spirit as its origin and peace as its binding force" (Eph 4:1, 3).

St. Augustine's heart was also aflame with Paul's conviction of humanity's new captivity in Christ: "Today our Lord Jesus Christ ascended into heaven; let our hearts ascend with him. . . . For just as he remained with us after his ascension, so we too are already in heaven with him, even though what is promised us has not yet been fulfilled in our bodies."[52]

St. Augustine could not have been more explicit: "We too are already in heaven with him." All that remains of our "not yet" presence in heaven is for us to "fill up what is lacking in the sufferings of Christ for the sake of his body, the Church" (Col 1:24). Jesus became our earthly existence so that he might carry the cross of humanity's longing to die to the captivity of this world's perishability. From this dying God raises us up that we might "fill up what is lacking in the [resurrection] of Christ." In that resurrection we become the imperishability of the new captivity for all eternity.

Is it far-fetched to believe that all of heaven is in our midst, now? Is the Lord's Prayer also far-fetched when we pray, "Thy kingdom come, thy will be done on earth as it is in heaven"? Our oneness with Christ is such that it is not far-fetched to believe that we are in heaven in Christ, as Christ is in our humanity on earth. St. Augustine exclaims: "No one but Christ descended and no one but Christ ascended; not because there is no distinction between the head and the body, but because the body as a unity cannot be separated from the head."[53]

Ascension's mystery contains the reason for human dignity. It enables us to understand more clearly why respect for life is imperative for human dignity. The worth of every human being is based on the sacredness of humanity's ascended presence in heaven with Christ as head of its body. In Christ, then, our humanity is the new captivity whose liberation we share. We are one with Christ and Christ is one with us. That oneness in heaven is the basis for the sanctity of human life.

The Feast of the Ascension is not a filler between Easter and Pentecost. Rather, the mystery of Christ's ascension bonds Easter and Pentecost. Like Easter, it proclaims the paschal mystery whereby we "fill up what is lacking" in the death and resurrection of Jesus. Like Pentecost, Christ's ascension heralds the Spirit of God whose descent into our lives returned Christ's risen presence to earth, freeing us for heaven's presence. This bonding of heaven and earth moves St. Paul to exhort: "You must lay aside your former way of life and the old self which deteriorates through illusion and desire, and acquire a fresh, spiritual way of thinking. You must put on that new man created in God's image, whose justice and holiness are born of truth" (Eph 4:22-24).

QUESTIONS FOR YOUR REFLECTION

1. Marriage is a way of life. How can one be fully wedded after giving consent to the other, yet not be fully married? By comparison, how can one be "already" in heaven but "not yet" in heaven?

2. In what sense are we the new captivity of Christ? When is captivity demeaning? When is captivity elevating?

3. How does the ascension of Christ unite the mysteries of Easter and Pentecost?

FRIDAY OF THE SIXTH WEEK

Transcendence Is Why We're Here

WORD

"For such is the power of great minds, such is the light of truly believing souls, that they put unhesitating faith in what is not seen with the bodily eye; they fix their desires on what is beyond sight. Such fidelity could never be born in our hearts, nor could anyone be justified by faith, if our salvation lay only in what was visible" (St. Leo the Great, pope).[54]

REFLECTION

An old song begins "Everyone wants to go to heaven, but no one wants to die!" A parody on that song might begin "Everybody wants transcendence, but no one cares what it means." Yes, God created every human being to climb above and fully share an existence beyond this world's. Whether we realize it or not, our longing for transcendence is why our hearts are restless. Transcendence is really what "everybody wants," but "no one cares what it means." Why? Because "no one wants to die" to this world's perishability.

I hazard the guess that one of the reasons we find the mysteries of Christ difficult to understand is because they point to the transcendence we may not want to understand. They are about an existence that lies *beyond* the perishable realities to which human purpose obliges us to die. The mystery of Christ's ascension makes no sense to people who either deny that transcendence exists or are true believers in this world's claim that "it doesn't get any better than this." For people who follow this line, why should they care what transcendence means? Who wants to die?

The human mind can experience the conviction of transcendence because it can utilize God's gift of faith. By way of faith the human mind can know the meaning of transcendence when illusions of this world's grandeur do not obstruct faith's light. The strangeness that accompanies transcendence may be, ironically, God's invitation to explore the mysteries of Christ and *transcend* the illusion of happiness our perishables pretend.

The power of this world's illusion of grandeur can be seen in the way it implants fear. Those who fear losing their possessions give evidence of the viselike hold with which this world's spirit keeps people captive. The failure to be in touch with transcendence leaves only the harvest of fear. This harvest will always be abundant because the world's pretense of transcendence is as perishable as its possessions.

Faith offers us the hope—the certainty— that Christ's ascension has elevated us to dwell far beyond the fear of losing this world's possessions. St. Leo the Great observes that "faith was increased by the Lord's Ascension and strengthened by the gift of the Spirit; it . . . remain[s] unshaken by fetters and imprisonment, exile and hunger, fires and raving beasts, and the most refined tortures ever devised by brutal persecutors."[55] Impregnable as this world's illusions may appear, they inevitably crumble in the face of the hope whose certainty puts us in touch with transcendence.

St. John the Evangelist declares:

> Everyone who has this hope based on [God]
> keeps himself pure, as he is pure (1 John 3:3).

In the eyes of God, the pure of heart are those whose lives are completely free of the illusion that this world's possessions grant them a glory commensurate with the dignity of the transcendence for which we have been created. The "pure" are those who really understand St. Paul's vision of life: "For, to me, 'life' means Christ" (Phil 1:21). Paul's certainty that "life means Christ" is the touch of transcendence.

Although we are called to an eternity of transcendence, the Church never forgets that all of us must temporarily dwell in the midst of this world's perishability. She acknowledges this truth by her use of possessions that, ironically, call us to be in touch with transcendence. Perishable as they are, the goods of this world are used as sacramentals, the understanding of which enables us to ascend to their imperishable meaning. "Our Redeemer's visible presence has passed into the sacraments," writes St. Leo the Great. "Our faith is nobler and stronger because sight has been replaced by a doctrine whose authority is accepted by believing hearts, enlightened from on high."[56]

Ascension's mystery invites us to believe that we already live in transcendence. Our presence with Christ and in Christ before the throne of God lacks only the purity that finds us free of this world's illusions of God-likeness. We are poor in spirit when our hearts have been cleansed of clingings to this world's spirit. These are the clingings that blind us to transcendence. As long as we fear the loss of our possessions, we shall always crave the illusion of their transcendence. It's like the song says, "Everybody wants to go to heaven, but nobody wants to die!"

QUESTIONS FOR YOUR REFLECTION

1. How does fear play a role in modern advertising? What do TV ads want us to fear? Why do they want us to fear?

2. The word "purity" is usually associated with sexuality. How is this single-issue approach to the word little more than an escape from purity's larger implications? What is the fullest meaning of purity in terms of our call to transcendence?

3. How does faith silence this world's claims that earthly possessions can enable us to "live happily ever after"?

Life Is Like a Flowing River

WORD

"That we have passed from death to life we know
because we love the brothers.
The way we came to understand love
was that he laid down his life for us;
we too must lay down our lives for the brothers" (1 John 3:14,
16).

REFLECTION

Nothing is more tragic than the shortsightedness of viewing life only
as earthly existence. St. Augustine writes insightfully of life's fullest
panorama:

> The Church recognizes two kinds of life as having been commended
> to her by God. One is a life of faith, the other is a life of vision;
> one is a life passed on pilgrimage in time, the other is a dwelling
> place in eternity; one is a life of toil, the other a life of repose; one
> is spent on the road, the other in our homeland; one is active, in-
> volving labor, the other contemplative, the reward of labor.[57]

St. Augustine views life's presence in this world as temporary and
incomplete. This world's existence does not represent the wholeness
of life that God intends for it to enjoy forever. Like a river that appears
briefly from around one bend only to disappear around another, our
lives here upon earth are but the tiniest portion of life's wholeness. The
psalmist observes:

> For a thousand years in your sight
> > are as yesterday, now that it is past,
> > or as a watch in the night (Ps 90:4).

Faith's perspective of life's wholeness beyond the perspective of our
earthly capacity to view it enables us to live this world's portion of life
in a much different way. The story of Cain and Abel is a good example
(see Gen 4:1-16). At the heart of that story is the shortsightedness of

Cain's perspective of earthly existence. His vision of human life becomes his focus. It is interesting that when the Genesis author of this story describes Cain's gift, he writes only that Cain "brought an offering to the Lord God from the fruit of the soil" (Gen 4:3).

Abel's perspective extends well beyond Cain's. The story continues, "Abel, for his part, brought one of the best firstlings of his flock." (Gen 4:4). Abel gives to God a "best" because his vision of life reaches beyond the perishability of this world's goodness. Abel's gift to God measures the largesse by which he views all of life. His view of life's wholeness is of an excellence that exceeds the "best" of his possessions.

There is little doubt that Cain planned to murder his brother because his myopic view of life could not coexist with Abel's faith perspective. It was God's recognition of Abel's faith that infuriated Cain. "The LORD looked with favor on Abel and his offering, but on Cain and his offering he did not. Cain greatly resented this and was crestfallen" (Gen 4:4-5). His resentment led him to the murder of his brother.

Clearly, Abel's gift acknowledged his faith in life's wholeness. He loved its wholeness more than the "firstlings" of this world's perishable excellence. His faith in life "around the bends" of life's earthly portion allowed him to acknowledge God's dominion over all of life with "the best firstlings of his flock."

Abel's perspective of life does not sit well with people whose short-range views have put them solely within the borders of that range. St. John testifies to this assertion:

> No need . . . to be surprised if the world hates you.
> That we have passed from death to life we know
> because we love the brothers. . . .
> The way we came to understand love
> was that he laid down his life for us;
> we too must lay down our lives for our brothers (1 John 3:13-14, 16).

Cain killed Abel because it was obvious that Abel's faith witnessed a love that carried him beyond Cain's short-range view of life. Abel's love carried him into the bosom of human life's ultimate purpose—communion with God. This is what inspired Abel to part with the "best firstlings of his flock." It is also the communion for which God raised our humanity from the dead. The resurrection of Jesus is God's good news that all of humanity possesses the dignity of God. When faith enables us to believe that, we shall never again be afraid to part with our "firstlings" for the life that lies "around the bend."

QUESTIONS FOR YOUR REFLECTION

1. Abortion and euthanasia have been favored at the highest level of this nation's tribunal of jurisprudence since 1973. How is this the evidence of a nation's shortsightedness which identifies the wholeness of human life solely from this world's perspective of its usefulness?

2. Why did St. John say that we need not "be surprised if the world hates [us]"?

3. How does our practice of sacrifice reveal our perspective about what constitutes the wholeness of human life?

SEVENTH SUNDAY OF EASTER

What's in a Name?

WORD

"His commandment is this:
we are to believe in the name of his Son, Jesus Christ,
and are to love one another as he commanded us.
Those who keep his commandments remain in him
*   and he in them.*
And this is how we know that he remains in us:
from the Spirit that he gave us" (1 John 3:23-24).

REFLECTION

The careful naming of children springs from a parental desire to bless them with the meaning of their names. For example, to name a child in memory of one whose life made a wholesome difference in the world is to invoke the power and the blessing of that difference.

Names represent more than infatuation with their sound. They represent the power of the goodness which each human being is capable of revealing to the world. When children are named after those whose lives touched others with goodness, beauty, and truth, they can be challenged to live those attributes. When they accept the meaning of their names, they have the power to evoke their transforming effects.

Very early in life I asked my mother the meaning of my name, John. "The Lord is gracious," came her prompt reply. Puzzled, I asked, "But what does that mean to me?" "Well," she began, "I hope your life will be a grace both for you and for others around you." She continued, "God's grace is really the presence of God's love of which I hope you will always be a sign. That's what your name means to me." The conversation ended but not the power of its teaching moment. From then on I saw my identity in a new light. The meaning of my name evoked an awareness of the destiny that carried me along paths which I might not otherwise have considered as a way of life.

The name of Jesus, "Savior," is the power of Jesus. His name restores all who hear his voice to the oneness that enables humankind to realize the God-likeness of humanity's purpose of existence. We are called to the intimacy of love which bonds the Father, Son, and Holy Spirit as the very identity of God. "God is love" (1 John 4:16), and we have been created to bear witness to the oneness whose love witnesses God's identity to the world. The witness of that identity is what salvation is.

The name of Jesus, then, is the imperative whereby we assent to the name that means salvation and consent to its power of achieving it. These two imperatives of assent and consent to the name of Jesus make us ready for the transformation by which we become witnesses of the love that is God's identity. We believe "in the name of . . . Jesus Christ, and are to love one another as he commanded us" (1 John 3:23).

St. Gregory of Nyssa observes: "When love has entirely cast out fear, and fear has been transformed into love, then the unity brought us by our Savior will be fully realized, for all men to be united with one another through their union with the one supreme Good."[58]

At every age the Holy Spirit continues to make available to us the saving power of Jesus' name. The passover of that name from Jesus' identity to ours is likewise the passover of God's glory to us. God's glory is the "weight" of divinity's triune identity, unceasingly calling us to the oneness that transforms us into the likeness of God. In the company of the Holy Spirit we travel on a pilgrimage that takes us before the throne of God, where we stand in the name of Christ.

Our purpose in this life is clear. We have been baptized to pass over from this world's identity to the identity of Jesus. Step by step we walk in the Spirit so that Jesus' name may fully transform us into the likeness we were created to become. It is when God and humankind are one that Christ's saving name ushers us into the full presence of God's friendship:

"I no longer speak of you as slaves, . . .
Instead, I call you friends,
since I have made known to you all that I heard from my Father"
(John 15:15).

That friendship is achieved through the power of Jesus' name. Friendship with God is what "Savior" means.

QUESTIONS FOR YOUR REFLECTION

1. What is your first name? What does it mean? What is the way of life to which your name calls you?

2. The name "Jesus" means "Savior." What is the salvation to which the name Jesus invites us to assent and consent? How do healing, reconciliation, forgiveness, and peacemaking relate to the name of Jesus, "Savior"?

3. In what way is true love the exercise of the power contained in the name of Jesus?

4. What is the role of the Holy Spirit in the bonding power of Jesus' name?

Seeing God Is Impossible. Really?

WORD

"This is how you can recognize God's Spirit:
every spirit that acknowledges Jesus Christ come in the flesh
belongs to God" (1 John 4:2).

REFLECTION

This chapter's title is an invitation to reflect on the utterly simple truth that Jesus Christ put all of humanity in touch with God. Before his coming this was the impossibility that Moses heard from God: "My face you cannot see, for no [one] sees me and still lives" (Exod 33:20).

These words have the appearance of a dilemma. On the one hand we have God's word that it is impossible to see God, and on the other we are faced with the imperative that we be in touch with God before we die. We are faced with a question: Does God command us to stake our lives on the foundation of an impossibility? Thanks be to God, the answer is no!

The imperative of humanly relating to God became a reality when God sent Jesus clothed in humanity's flesh and blood. In him the fullness of God became visible so that all of humankind might be able to see, hear, taste, and touch the invisibility of God. In so doing, Jesus' coming raised all of creation to the dignity of being sacraments that reveal God's invisibility. St. Paul writes: "Since the creation of the world, invisible realities, God's eternal power and divinity, have become visible, recognized through the things he has made" (Rom 1:20).

St. John cautions his readers not to trust the "many false prophets" whose teachings leave unacknowledged the presence of God "in the flesh." He is emphatic. No spirit is of God when its alleged claims are inconsistent with God's embodiment in creation. He writes:

> This is how you can recognize God's Spirit:
> every spirit that acknowledges Jesus Christ come in the flesh
> belongs to God,
> while every spirit that fails to acknowledge him
> does not belong to God (1 John 4:2-3).

In St. John's teaching, the "bottom line" issue of Christ's incarnation is its fulfillment of what humankind once found impossible. Christ's incarnation fills the whole world with "God's Grandeur," awaiting only the ackowledgment of faith.

Jesus taught in a way that was consistent with his human identity. His words about God's invisible reality were clothed in images the people understood. Whatever he could see, hear, taste, and touch were the embodiments—sacraments—of God's presence. Seeds, salt, water, birds of the air, little children, lost coins, lost sheep, lost sons, were raised

115

by Christ to the dignity of sacramentality. He made it possible for everyone to embrace with faith the God Moses could not see with his eyes.

To the Samaritan woman at the well, Jesus elevated water to the sacramentality that enabled her to quench her thirst for the intimacy of God's love. Jesus said: "The water I give . . . shall become a fountain within . . . leaping up to provide eternal life" (John 4:14). About this, St. Cyril of Jerusalem observes to his catechumens: "Why did Christ call the grace of the Spirit water? [Because] it adapts itself to the needs of every creature that receives it."[59]

The incarnation of Christ is more than a theological formulation. It is "the way" by which we can journey in the world's perishability, graced to reveal the imperishability of God's identity. All of God's creatures groan for our acknowledgment of their sacramentality. To acknowledge creation's embodiment of God's awesome presence is to liberate it from the futility to which our blindness has made it captive (see Rom 8:19-21).

Today our polluted environment offers evidence of creation's groanings to be freed from the futility of consumerism. But these groanings are faint cries compared to humanity's never-ending thirst to be quenched only by God. We, too, groan to be embraced by the Godlikeness we were created to share for all eternity.

The groanings of both creation and humanity can be quenched when faith, hope, and love are reverently acknowledged as the entries of Christ's presence in the sacramentality of all creation. This acknowledgment is the gift of God's Holy Spirit who, like an inexhaustible fountain of living water, unites us to God and to one another. "Every spirit that acknowledges Jesus Christ come in [creation] belongs to God."

Is seeing God impossible? Not really!

QUESTIONS FOR YOUR REFLECTION

1. How did Jesus transform the impossibility of seeing God into the reality of beholding him?

2. In what way do the seven sacraments proclaim the sacramentality of all creation?

3. When you ask a priest to bless an article, what are you really acknowledging?

4. To what captivity does all self-indulgence bind God's creation? To what futility does consumerism bind us?

116

"You're Nobody 'Til Somebody Loves You"

WORD

"If God has loved us so,
we must have the same love for one another. . . .
When anyone acknowledges that Jesus is the Son of God,
God dwells in him
and he in God. . . .
God is love,
and he who abides in love
abides in God,
and God in him" (1 John 4: 11, 15, 16).

REFLECTION

To acknowledge another's presence goes much deeper than merely acknowledging physical presence. Acknowledgment of presence is the recognition that someone's life has made a difference. When a person has helped another to experience the meaning of love, that person has been fully acknowledged and recognized. As the title of the song suggests, "You're nobody 'til somebody loves you."

St. John the Evangelist exhorts Christians to give Jesus Christ the acknowledgment that recognizes the power of his love in their lives:

When anyone acknowledges that Jesus is the Son of God,
God dwells in him
and he in God.

This acknowledgment, rooted in faith, enables us to live our lives persuaded that the name of Jesus integrates us with God and with one another. To believe that Jesus' name represents life's saving purpose is to acknowledge that he is in our midst, making us one with God and with all others. To acknowledge Jesus as the source of our integration with God and humankind is to open our lives to the Holy Spirit's transforming power. That makes a difference! St. John asserts:

> The way we know we remain in him
> and he in us
> is that he has given us his Spirit (1 John 4:13).

God's Spirit was sent to make effective in each of us the integrating power of Jesus' mission. To acknowledge Jesus Christ is to surrender ourselves to God's Spirit, who is within us to complete the mission of Jesus' saving name "Savior." Merely to give a nod of assent without the consent to share in the Spirit's work of salvation is to display inconsistency. St. John minces no words:

> If anyone says, "My love is fixed on God,"
> yet hates his brother,
> he is a liar.
> One who has no love for the brother he has seen
> cannot love the God he has not seen.
> The commandment we have from him is this:
> Whoever loves God must also love his brother (1 John 4:20-21).

Must love his brother? Yes! "God is love!" There are not two loves because there are not two Gods. Love is indivisible because God is indivisible. There is not a love reserved for God and a love reserved for others. Love is one! Failure to acknowledge oneness is to live the life of liars whose expertise is inconsistency.

We have previously noted that consistency between what we say we believe and how we live what we say is integrity. When our lives are marked with integrity, we enjoy the wholeness indispensible for our transformation into the likeness of God. The integrating power of the Holy Spirit becomes effective in the lives of those who give evidence of integrity.

"Wholeness is holiness" is the theme of a small book. The author insists that we are not made holy by a heavenly gift that has no relationship with the human processes of becoming wholly human. As the Word of God came into our flesh by way of Mary's integrity of personhood, so the integrating power of Jesus' name continues to be enfleshed within the context of our integrity, that is, wholeness with God, others, and ourselves. To acknowledge this under the guidance of the Holy Spirit is to lead a life of holiness. That makes a difference!

Are the holy only a few? St. Basil reflects:

> The Spirit is the Source of holiness, a spiritual light, and he offers
> his own light to every mind to help it in its search for truth. By

nature the Spirit is beyond the reach of our mind, but we can know him by his goodness. The power of the Spirit fills the whole universe, but he gives himself only to those who are worthy, acting in each according to the measure of his faith.[60]

Who are these "worthy" ones? In the mind of God, *all* are worthy of becoming the image and likeness of God. The issue is not whether God has selected some and rejected others. The issue is not whether God wants a few to be in heaven. In Christ, all of us are already there! The issue is, do we want to live the implications of our presence with the ascended Christ? Do we want the integrity of becoming who we say we are? Do we want to witness the life we say that God is? To answer yes to these questions is to be found "worthy" of being acknowledged by God's Spirit. Indeed, you're somebody when God's Spirit loves you! That makes *the* difference!

QUESTIONS FOR YOUR REFLECTION

1. Two persons who consent to wed display an acknowledgment of each other's personhood at a level that acknowledges the difference each person has already meant. How does that acknowledgment at the wedding carry over into the marriage?

2. What is the difference between our assent to Christ's message and our consent to it? Which of the two is the dynamic of evangelization? Which of the two leads to conversion?

3. Why is lying the basis of one's lack of integrity? What is the truth that makes integrity a reality?

Three Stages of One Pilgrimage

WORD

"Jesus Christ it is who came through water and blood—
not in water only,
but in water and in blood.
It is the Spirit who testifies to this,
and the Spirit is truth.
Thus there are three that testify,
the Spirit and the water and the blood—
and these three are of one accord" (1 John 5:6-8).

REFLECTION

In her beginnings the Church welcomed new members by means of the catechumenate. During long periods of experiencing the shared faith of the Church's family, seekers of ecclesial companionship were led, stage by stage, toward the wholeness that bonded them with God and the Church. Today, the catechumenate has been restored for those who hunger and thirst for the belonging, the oneness, and the intimacy that justifies the Church's celebration of human purpose.

The catechumenal process is a pilgrimage experience. In her beginnings the Church was described as "the way" by which seekers of truth and life journeyed toward their destiny. Pope John Paul II's first encyclical cites the journey of each human being as the "one single way" in which the Church unites herself with Christ on his ongoing Passover experience. The Holy Father clearly states:

> When we penetrate by means of the continually and rapidly increasing experience of the human family into the mystery of Jesus Christ, we understand with greater clarity that there is at the basis of all these ways . . . one single way . . . Christ the Lord [who by] "his Incarnation . . . united himself with each man" (*Gaudium et Spes*, 22). The Church wishes to serve this single end: that each person may be able to find Christ so that Christ may walk with each person along the path of life, with the power of the truth about man and the world. . . .[61]

"One single way"? Yes, because Jesus came to be *the* way, befitting the dignity which God created all men and women to enjoy. Jesus came clothed with our humanity so that he might be for us the "way" of the Passover pilgrimage. In a very real sense, Jesus was and is humankind's catechumenal experience. Stage by stage he traced out for us the pilgrimage that all of us must travel as we surrender ourselves to the destiny that God designed for our happiness. With Christ each of us passes over from the lie that acknowledges only this world's spirit as worth possessing to the joy of embracing Jesus Christ, humanity's dignity worth becoming.

What is the "catechumenate" of Christ's Passover mystery? St. John describes three stages of Christ's "way":

> The Spirit and the water and the blood—
> and these three are of one accord.

In each of these stages—Spirit, water, and blood—there is the testimony that Christ's Passover pilgrimage is our way, our truth, and our life. He traveled that pilgrimage clothed with our humanity that we might be eternally clothed with God's divinity. He lived in our midst to call us to these three stages of his human catechumenal experience so that we might enjoy the peace of his companionship: of *water,* that we might be aware of the baptismal commitment to follow Christ cleansed of any clinging to this world's spirit; of *blood,* that we might wholeheartedly embrace the cross which is the lived experience of baptism's commitment; of *Spirit,* that we might surrender to the Holy Spirit's witness of Christ's risen presence in a world of empty claims and promises.

This catechumenal pilgrimage of water, blood, and Spirit ends only when we take our last breath. When these three stages of Christ's catechumenal "way" have been the "one single way" of our lives, fear will not occupy the center of our lives. The presence of Christ will fill with love the many rooms in the hiddenness of our lives. St. John writes:

> Our love is brought to perfection in this,
> that we should have confidence on the day of judgment;
> for our relation to this world is just like his.
> Love has no room for fear (1 John 4:17-18).

QUESTIONS FOR YOUR REFLECTION

1. What is the likeness between the way we became members of our families and the catechumenal way in which the Church invites us to become members of her family?

2. For all who have become members of the Church, in what way do the seven sacraments celebrate a catechumenal "way" for our daily lives?

3. Can there really be a "baptism in the Spirit" without our experience of the baptism "of water" or "of blood"?

4. What is the evidence that the spirit of the flesh is at our life's center (see Gal 5:19-20)? What is the evidence that God's Spirit is at the center of our lives (see Gal 5:22-23)?

THURSDAY OF THE SEVENTH WEEK

Strength Through Leaving

WORD

"After Christ had completed his mission on earth, it still remained necessary for us to become sharers in the divine nature of the Word. We had to give up our own life and be so transformed that we would begin to live an entirely new kind of life. . . . This was something we could do only by sharing in the Holy Spirit" (St. Cyril of Alexandria, bishop).[62]

REFLECTION

When life's meaning is confined to physical presence, the pain of separation from loved ones takes us to the brink of bitterness. To define love and life solely by physical presence gives evidence that one has failed to see beyond this world's definition of human meaning. To ignore a higher meaning of human life makes the pain of separation unbearable.

Physical presence is not the fullest meaning of human existence. For the sake of peace in times of grief it is imperative that we understand this. Any reflection on the mystery of Christ's ascension and his sending of the Holy Spirit is little more than an academic exercise for those whose search for love and life never extends beyond this world's kingdom of perishables. Jesus insisted that his physical presence was not the ultimate reason for his coming when he said:

"If I fail to go,
the Paraclete will never come to you,
whereas if I go,
I will send him to you. . . .
When he comes . . .
he will guide you to all truth" (John 16:7, 13).

The physical presence of Jesus opened the door to a mission that lay beyond humanity's earthly capability of achieving. He came to announce the good news that God's Spirit-presence would come to fill the whole world regardless of earthly limitations of time and space. The coming of the Holy Spirit enables all of humanity to share in the presence of God's life. Jesus sent the Holy Spirit to dwell in the deepest regions of humankind's being, where communion with God and one another takes place. Jesus sent God's Spirit to transform our identities, a transformation that Jesus acknowledged as beyond his earthly capacity to achieve:

"I tell you the sober truth:
It is much better for you that I go.
If I fail to go,
the Paraclete will never come to you" (John 16:7).

St. Cyril of Alexandria comments on this: "As long as Christ . . . was in the flesh, it must have seemed to believers that they possessed every blessing in him; but when the time came for him to ascend to the heavenly Father, it was necessary for him to be united through his Spirit to those who worshiped him, and to dwell in our hearts through faith."[63]

God wills that we measure human meaning by standards that lie *outside* our sense experience. Why? Because human meaning points to an existence that is imperishable. God wills that we seek for the imperishability which cannot be measured by this world's instruments of measuring human dignity. It is "through faith" that we accept what we cannot measure and open ourselves to the transforming power of God's Spirit-presence. "May Christ dwell in your hearts through faith," St. Paul writes, "[that] you will be able to grasp fully, with all the holy ones the breadth and length and height and depth of Christ's love . . . to him whose power . . . can do immeasurably more than we ask or imagine" (Eph 3:17-18, 20). Yes, immeasurably more!

On Pentecost God's will was fully expressed. Jesus' physical presence had given way to God's Spirit-presence. The Holy Spirit came to restore Christ's physical presence *in his followers.* From that Pentecost moment, the disciples never again looked back with nostalgia on Jesus' physical presence. Pentecost proclaimed the good news that Christ's risen presence is in us, with us, and through us. The New Testament echoes Pentecost's proclamation that we have the dignity of being the incarnation of Christ's earthly presence until the end of time. Speaking to his disciples for the last time as he ascended into heaven, he said:

> "Go, therefore, and make disciples of all the nations.
> Baptize them in the name
> of the Father,
> and of the Son,
> and of the Holy Spirit.
> Teach them to carry out everything I have commanded you.
> And know that I am with you always, until the end of the world!"
> (Matt 28:19-20).

QUESTIONS FOR YOUR REFLECTION

1. The title of this reflection suggests that there is strength in separation. What is that strength and how does faith enable us to accept separation's pain?

2. Why did Jesus insist that he must leave this world?

3. What is our role in enabling Jesus to be physically present "until the end of the world"?

4. Why is there no evidence in the New Testament of any nostalgia for Jesus' physical presence?

5. What is the Eucharist's sacramental presence saying to us in terms of our dignity to be the body of Christ here upon earth?

Let There Be Light

WORD

"We receive the Spirit of truth so that we can know the things of God" (St. Hilary, bishop).[64]

REFLECTION

On a very cold, sunny day, a bit of darkness became a permanent fixture in my right eye. Without warning, a "flashbulb" explosion of light ended the entry of all light through the eye's center. Its vision now is little more than peripheral.

Curiously, my partial blindness has been a blessing. The absence of light in the center of my eye has enlightened my understanding of the Holy Spirit's role in the center of our lives. This is what I mean: The failure of light to facilitate center vision has led me to understand that the Holy Spirit is the light that enables all of us to focus on the "center vision" of humanity's meaning. St. Hilary writes that "unless [the soul] absorbs the gift of the Spirit through faith, the mind . . . lacks the light necessary for that knowledge."[65]

The experience of partial blindness has graced me to understand that God's Spirit offers the light that we may see more clearly the way, the truth, and the life God marks out for us in the darkness of this world's "light." I am constantly reminded that God's Spirit does not present us with answers and solutions to problems. Rather, God's Spirit is the light that offers us the opportunity to see precisely who we are and what God has called us to become.

God's Spirit neither removes error from the world nor our freedom to choose it. But God's Spirit offers us the light by which we can see both the error and its frightening implications. We are Spirit-led to see clearly that Christ's risen presence is the central meaning of human existence. My loss of center vision has, ironically, enabled me to understand Christ as the center of life, without which all of life is lived on the periphery.

The Spirit guides us to choose Christ, whose life is the light and center of human purpose. The "progressives" who ignore our rootedness in Christ promote the radicalism that places us on the periphery of human existence. St. John warns his readers, "Anyone who is so 'progressive' that he does not remain rooted in the teaching of Christ does not possess God, while anyone who remains rooted in the teaching [of Christ] possesses both the Father and the Son" (2 John 9).

God created light first so that all men and women might see that they share in the work of forming the beauty and the goodness of creation. This call to share in God's work of creation was offered to humankind again on Pentecost. On that day there came into the world a noise like a strong driving wind and tongues of fire that parted and came to rest on Christ's disciples (see Acts 2:1-3). God's Spirit came as the light of our never-ending Pentecost experience, by which we can "know the things of God" in both the storms and the radiance of daily living.

We are an ascension people, Eastered by the hope that our lives are secure as we follow Pentecost's pilgrimage led by the Holy Spirit's "column of light." Pentecost's light radiates from the tongues of fire that enlighten the darkness around us. These tongues of fire guide us to God's work of transformation. Unceasingly, the Holy Spirit calls us to be columns of light in the world.

We near the end of Easter's remembrance of Christ's paschal pilgrimage of death and resurrection. We prepare to celebrate the Holy Spirit's call to embrace the reality of that Passover mystery. In the storms and joys of our lives, we are called to "fill up what is lacking in the sufferings [and resurrection] of Christ for the sake of his body, the church" (Col 1:24). Christ lacking? No, we are lacking. We lack the poverty of spirit in which God's Spirit calls us to live the dying and rising of Christ in our humanity so that we might become the fullness of humanity's destiny through the light of the Holy Spirit.

QUESTIONS FOR YOUR REFLECTION

1. What is your most painful cross? How can this cross become the blessing of Christ's ongoing resurrection? What is the role of the Holy Spirit as we make our passover pilgrimage of dying and rising?

2. How is a spirituality that seeks from God precise answers to personal and social problems a problem for faith? In what way is the Holy Spirit the light rather than the answer for our problems?

3. How is the image of light a key to our deeper understanding of the Holy Spirit's identity?

4. The seven gifts of the Holy Spirit are wisdom, understanding, knowledge, counsel, piety, fortitude, and fear of the Lord. Wouldn't it be more enlightening to understand these gifts as fires that enlighten rather than as "things" to possess?

Love Is the Church's Language of Unity

WORD

"The disciples spoke in the language of every nation. . . . It was love that was to bring the Church of God together all over the world. . . . So today the Church, united by the Holy Spirit, speaks in the language of every people" (sixth-century African author).[66]

REFLECTION

No illusion is more deceiving than the claim that uniformity is the mark of unity. This claim has been the position of those who insist that the use of Latin for Eucharistic worship is the hallmark of Church unity. They continue to cry out "heresy" as they behold the diversity of peoples gathering to praise God in their own tongues.

Unity's depth lies deeper in humankind's makeup than the tips of their tongues. To require one language with which to praise God is a sign of uniformity. But to speak one language from the hearts of many diversities is the sign of unity. Love is the language of the heart.

Love does not need to be translated for universal understanding. It needs only to be witnessed. Regardless of their cultural, political, sociological, and spiritual differences, all men and women recognize the language of love. This is the language that God spoke as the Holy Spirit's diversity of tongues came to inflame the hearts of Christ's followers.

The language of love is the only language that the Church has been commissioned to speak to many nations.

There are three ways in which the universal Church has been commissioned to speak the language of love. From the identity of Christ her founder, the Church has been sent to be the sign of Christ's Word, Christ's oneness with God and humankind, and Christ's servanthood for all men and women regardless of diversity. Like Christ, then, the Church is prophet, priest, and servant. To be this identity the Church needs only the language of love to carry out Christ's threefold mission.

Love must first speak justice, the language of prophets. No nation is devoid of a deep sense of what is right. The substance of justice is the rightness that exists between God and humankind. That rightness is about the identity God created all men and women to become. People of all times and places sense their kinship to an identity whose truth, beauty, and goodness they long to share with God. When that kinship is not recognized and is replaced by a kinship with this world's perishability, injustice and division become the language of the world.

A second way the Church speaks the language of love is to gather people for worship. The Church insists that worship is not the exercise of rituals without ritual's meaning. When love of ritual passes over to the love of people, all of the world's diversities will recognize the language she speaks. The sixth-century preacher cries out, "[Pentecost] will be no empty festival for you if you really live what you are celebrating."[67]

The living of ritual in daily life completes the worship it signifies. When people who live in the image and likeness of God's love gather around the altar to sacramentalize their love, worship becomes an effective witness of Christ's presence. St. John writes to one of his flocks, "It has given me great joy to have [you] bear witness to how truly you walk in the path of truth" (3 John 3).

A third way the Church speaks her language of love is to serve people precisely where they are diverse. To condemn people for their differences is to use one's own diversity as the universal model for what is right and wrong. When one's diversity seeks to replace all diversities, uniformity becomes unity's deformity. When the motivation to serve others is based solely on the likenesses to which we can relate with ease, then the authenticity of that motivation needs to be questioned because to love only those we like betrays the cross of Christ.

While it is not easy to serve diversity, it is, nevertheless, the substance of servanthood's role in speaking Christ's language of love. St. John writes: "You demonstrate fidelity by all that you do for [all] even though they are strangers; indeed, they have testified to your love before the church" (3 John 5-6). There are no strangers to the Church's language of love. This is the language that speaks catholicity.

The Church is prophet, priest, and servant. This is the context for the love that speaks to all tongues and rituals. This is the language that evangelizes as it draws diversity into one body whose language of one heart is easily understood by all. "By this spectacular miracle," exclaims the sixth-century homilist, "[the disciples] became a sign of the Catholic Church, which embraces the language of every nation. . . . The Church is the house of God, built up of living stones whose master is almighty God."[68]

QUESTIONS FOR YOUR REFLECTION

1. Why does the language of love need no translation for recognition and understanding?

2. To be genuinely prophetic is to "speak God." How, then, is love prophetic? How does love relate to justice?

3. When mere ritual performance is regarded as the only imperative for the celebration of sacraments, how does that explain the ineffectiveness of sacraments? How does mere performance of ritual explain the complaint that "I don't get anything out of Mass"?

4. To what universal likeness are we blind when we reach out only to people whose likenesses to ours are the conditions for our help?

Now the Ball Is in Your Court

WORD

*"It is our duty to use the coin committed to our charge
and make it yield a rich profit for the Lord"* (St. Irenaeus,
bishop).[69]

REFLECTION

My newly purchased computer and printer were finally delivered.
When I signed for the merchandise, the deliveryman departed with a
quip and a wink, "The ball is in your court now!"

My heart sank. Piled before me were three large boxes of mystery
complete with software and directions. As I read the directions, I found
myself more deeply entrenched in mystery. I needed guidance, and
thanks to a fellow priest, the hiddenness of the computer's mystery un-
folded.

Pentecost Sunday never fails to remind me of the deliveryman's
parting words, "The ball is in your court now." This festive day charges
us to give form and shape to the mysteries of Christ which we celebrate. From Advent until Easter, the Church carefully spells out directions that guide us to the way, truth, and life of our earthly pilgrimage
toward life's meaning. Along with the directions, the Feast of Pentecost renews the hope that God's Spirit is with us as we assemble our
lives according to Christ's directions. Jesus said to his disciples:

> "The Paraclete, the Holy Spirit
> whom the Father will send in my name,
> will instruct you in everything,
> and remind you of all that I told you" (John 14:26).

No, Christ's ascension did not leave us alone with the ball in our court.
Jesus promised his disciples, "I will not leave you orphaned; I will come
back to you" (John 14:18). The presence of God's Spirit, who guides
us to enflesh the mysteries of faith, is the reason we gather to celebrate
Pentecost's mystery.

But we must not forget that the ball is *still* in our court. Pentecost's feast makes it clear that God's Spirit came in tongues of fire "to rest on each of them" (Acts 2:3) so that the disciples might be enlightened to carry on Christ's redemptive mission. The presumption that the Holy Spirit will "make all of the scores" is as hopeless as the extreme of despair.

When Jesus gathered his disciples for a last meal together, he identified himself with bread and wine. As he broke the bread and passed the cup, he asked them to "do this in remembrance of me" (1 Cor 11:24). Do what? To break the bread of their lives and shed their blood as testimony that God's Spirit is re-membering the presence of Christ. The reality of this re-membering of Christ in his ecclesial presence is what gives meaning to each Sunday's Eucharistic celebration of Easter and Pentecost.

Pentecost does not end an Advent-to-Easter presentation of the mysteries of faith. Advent, Christmas, Epiphany, Lent, Easter, Ascension, and Pentecost are not celebrations of mysteries for our admiration only. They are invitations for us to become what we celebrate. The mysteries of faith become visible in the flesh and blood of our presence. We give form to the meaning of their hiddenness.

The time between Pentecost and Advent is not "filler." These thirty-four weeks of Ordinary Time exhort us to live faith's mysteries so that Christ might be re-membered in his ecclesial body. Led by God's Spirit, our lived witness of faith makes visible the presence of Jesus in the world. The Spirit of Jesus is with us so that the truth of Jesus' promise might be continuously verified: "I will come back to you." The Holy Spirit is with us that we might become the "fifth gospel."

St. Irenaeus concludes the Lent and Easter presentation of Christ's paschal mystery with the image of a coin we have been given to invest. He challenges us "to use the coin committed to our charge and make it yield a rich profit for the Lord." Yes, it is one thing to have a coin, it is quite another to use it. Like coins inscribed with images, the paschal mystery is inscribed with the image of the Father, Son, and Holy Spirit. If we "use" the paschal mystery "for the Lord," the image of Christ's dying and rising will become visible on the face of the Church.

Pentecost speaks to us today: You have the directions with God's Spirit to guide you. Now the ball is in your court!

QUESTIONS FOR YOUR REFLECTION

1. Read the parable of the silver pieces (Matt 25:14-30). Why was the man with the one coin condemned? How does the parable relate to our role in the mystery of Pentecost?

2. What is the sigificance of the Holy Spirit's tongues of fire resting on the disciples? In what respect does this image present us with a grave obligation?

3. The French have a saying "noblesse oblige," that is, "nobility obliges." What is our nobility? Why does it obligate?

4. Why is the celebration of the Eucharist an obligation? What is the difference between remembering and re-membering?

Notes

1. St. Anastasius of Antioch, "A Discourse," *Patrologia Graeca*. See *Liturgy of the Hours* (New York: Catholic Book Publishing Company, 1976) 2:568.

2. "Jerusalem Catechesis," *Patrologia Graeca*. See *Liturgy of the Hours* 2:596.

3. *Ibid.* 2:608.

4. *Ibid.* 2:622.

5. Gerard Manley Hopkins, "God's Grandeur." See *Liturgy of the Hours* 2:1681.

6. "Jerusalem Catechesis," *Patrologia Graeca*. See *Liturgy of the Hours* 2:622.

7. Pseudo-Chrysostom, "Ancient Easter Homily," *Patrologia Graeca*." See *Liturgy of the Hours* 2:644.

8. Joseph Cardinal Bernardin, *A Consistent Ethic of Life* (Kansas City, Mo.: Sheed and Ward, 1988) 35.

9. St. Fulgentius, "A Book to Monimus," *Corpus Christianorum Series Latina*. See *Liturgy of the Hours* 2:653.

10. St. Leo the Great, "A Sermon on the Passion," *Patrolgia Latina*. See *Liturgy of the Hours* 2:660.

11. *Ibid.*

12. Bernardin, *A Consistent Ethic of Life* 61.

13. St. Theodore the Studite, "Sermon on the Adoration of the Cross," *Patrologia Graeca*. See *Liturgy of the Hours* 2:677.

14. St. Justin Martyr, "The First Apology in Defense of the Christians," *Patrologia Graeca*. See *Liturgy of the Hours* 2:694–95.

15. St. Augustine, "Sermon," *Corpus Christianorum Series Latina*. See *Liturgy of the Hours* 2:713.

16. *Ibid.*

17. St. Justin Martyr, "The First Apology in Defense of the Christians," *Quasten, Florilegium Patristicum*. See *Liturgy of the Hours* 2:719.

18. St. Iranaeus, "Against Heresies," *Sources Chretiennes*. See *Liturgy of the Hours* 2:728.

19. Sacramentary, Preface 77, Christian Death 1 (New York: Catholic Book Publishing Company, 1985).

20. St. Ephrem, "A Sermon Concerning Our Lord," *Opera edit. Lamy.* See *Liturgy of the Hours* 2:734.

21. Anthony de Mello, *The Heart of the Enlightened (New York: Doubleday, 1989) 13.*

22. Adela Yarbro Collins, *The Apocalypse* (Wilmington: Michael Glazier, 1982) 88.

23. St. Gregory the Great, "Homily on the Gospels," *Patrolgia Latina.* See *Liturgy of the Hours* 2:754.

24. St. Basil the Great, "On the Holy Spirit," *Sources Chretiennes.* See *Liturgy of the Hours* 2:762.

25. *Ibid.* 2:763.

26. St. Peter Chrysologus, "Sermon," *Patrologia Latina.* See *Liturgy of the Hours* 2:770.

27. *Ibid.* 2:772.

28. St. Hilary, "Treatise on the Trinity," *Patrologia Latina.* See *Liturgy of the Hours* 2:778.

29. *The Documents of Vatican II, The Church Today,* ed. Walter Abbott (New York: The America Press, 1966) no. 32.

30. St. Clement, "A Letter to the Corinthians," *Funk.* See *Liturgy of the Hours* 2:796.

31. Pope John Paul II, *To Men and Women Religious.* (Boston: Daughters of St. Paul) March 25, 1984, 4:9.

32. St. Cyril of Alexandria, "Commentary on the Letter to the Romans," *Patrologia Graeca.* See *Liturgy of the Hours* 2:806.

33. Sacramentary, Eucharistic Prayer of Reconciliation, app. VI. 1132.

34. St. Cyril of Alexandria, "Commentary on the Letter to the Romans," *Patrologia Graeca.* See *Liturgy of the Hours* 2:807.

35. St. Maximus of Turin, "Sermon," *Corpus Christianorum Series Latina.* See *Liturgy of the Hours* 2:816.

36. St. Gregory of Nyssa, "Sermon on the Resurrection of Christ," *Jaeger IX.* See *Liturgy of the Hours* 2:826.

37. St. Cyril of Alexandria, "A Commentary on the Gospel of John," *Patrologia Graeca.* See *Liturgy of the Hours* 2:833.

38. "A Letter to Diognetus," *Funk.* See *Liturgy of the Hours* 2:840.

39. "On Evangelization in the Modern World," no. 21 (Washington: Publications Office of the U.S. Catholic Conference, 1976) 17.

40. *Ibid.*

41. "A Letter to Diognetus," *Funk.* See *Liturgy of the Hours* 2:840.

42. St. Gaudentius of Brescia, "A Treatise," *Corpus Scriptorum Ecclesiasticorum Latinorum.* See *Liturgy of the Hours* 2:850.

43. Blessed Isaac of Stella, "Sermon," *Patrologia Latina.* See *Liturgy of the Hours* 2:856.

44. St. Augustine, "'Discourse on the Psalms," *Corpus Christianorum Series Latina*. See *Liturgy of the Hours* 2:684).

45. Sacramentary, Eucharistic Prayer II.

46. The Church in the Modern World, no. 5.

47. Didymus of Alexandria, "Treatise on the Trinity," *Patrologia Graeca*. See *Liturgy of the Hours* 2:882.

48. St. Cyril of Alexandria, "Commentary on the Gospel of John," *Patrologia Graeca*. See *Liturgy of the Hours* 2:890.

49. *Ibid.* 889.

50. *Ibid.* 889–90.

51. St. Leo the Great, "Sermon on the Ascension," *Patrologia Latina*. See *Liturgy of the Hours* 2:898.

52. St. Augustine, "Sermon on the Ascension," *Supplementum Patrologia Latina*. See *Liturgy of the Hours* 2:920–21.

53. *Ibid.* 922.

54. St. Leo the Great, "Sermon on the Ascension," *Patrologia Latina*. See *Liturgy of the Hours* 2:937.

55. *Ibid.*

56. *Ibid.* 938.

57. St. Augustine, "Sermon on the Ascension," *Supplementum Patrologia Latina*. See *Liturgy of the Hours* 2:920–21.

58. St. Gregory of Nyssa, "Song of Songs," *Jaeger VI*. See *Liturgy of the Hours* 2:957–58.

59. St. Cyril of Jerusalem, "Catechetical Instruction," *Patrologia Graeca*. See *Liturgy of the Hours* 2:966.

60. St. Basil the Great, "Treatise on the Holy Spirit," *Patrologia Graeca*. See *Liturgy of the Hours* 2:975.

61. Pope John Paul II, *Redemptor Hominis* (Washington: Publications Office of the U. S. Catholic Conference, 1979) 39–40.

62. St. Cyril of Alexandria, "Commentary on the Gospel of John," *Patrologia Graeca*. See *Liturgy of the Hours* 2:990.

63. *Ibid.*

64. St. Hilary, "On the Trinity," *Patologia Latina*. See *Liturgy of the Hours* 2:999.

65. *Ibid.*

66. Sixth-century African author, "Sermon," *Patrologia Latina*. See *Liturgy of the Hours* 2:1006.

67. *Ibid.* 1007.

68. *Ibid.* 1006–07.

69. St. Irenaeus, "Against Heresies," *Sources Chretiennes*. See *Liturgy of the Hours* 2:1026.